SILENT AWARENESS

The Revelation That Changes Everything

Cynthia Overweg

Foreword by Gabriele Uhlein, OSF, PhD

IN THE NOW
MEDIA

Published by
In the Now Media
P.O. Box 143
Oak View, California, 93022

Printed in the United States of America

SILENT AWARENESS: The Revelation That Changes Everything

Copyright © 2021 by Cynthia Overweg

First Edition 2021

Cover photograph by R.M. Nunes, i-Stock

Cover design by Eroll Muslija

Library of Congress Control Number: 2021907329

Meditation, Mindfulness, New Thought, Spirituality

ISBN: 978-0-578-76583-9 (paperback)
ISBN: 978-1-7370139-0-7 (e-book)
ISBN: 978-1-7370139-1-4 (hardcover)

Praise for SILENT AWARENESS

"One of the most difficult subjects to approach let alone write about is silence, a subject with no content, but one that, like the universe, contains it all. Cynthia Overweg's writing is classic literature, easy to read, and deeply moving. This is a book I couldn't stop reading because it took me so deeply inward."

— **R.E. Mark Lee,** author of *World Teacher: The Life and Teaching of J. Krishnamurti*

"In this wonderful book, Cynthia Overweg gives simple and practical suggestions which can help a searcher to be embraced by the Mysterious Silence pervading the whole cosmos. As she points out, this Silence, or Soundless Sound, has blessed the great sages, poets and musicians with love and delight. Highly recommended."

— **Ravi Ravindra, PhD,** author of *The Wisdom of Patañjali's Yoga*

"This serene, thoughtful, and meditative book helps calm the mind and open us to the stillness that underlies the world of substance."

— **Richard Smoley,** author of *Inner Christianity: A Guide to the Esoteric Tradition*

"Cynthia Overweg beautifully captures what it means to know who we are and how our lives are linked with all other lives, from the slightest fluttering of a leaf to the Ground of Being. She does this directly, just as it is, without words getting in the way. *Silent Awareness* will transform the way you see the world."

— **Robert Ellwood, PhD,** author of *Mysticism and Religion*

"*Silent Awareness* is exquisite. Nothing is missed in Cynthia Overweg's wise and inspiring book. She offers sensitive insight into the inner transformation that comes from deep listening and Sacred Silence."

— **Bridget Blomfield, PhD,** author of *The Language of Tears: My Journey into the World of Shi'i Muslim Women*

SILENT AWARENESS

*For Cor, whose wise and loving presence
makes everything possible.*

Contents

"Silence is the great revelation."

Lao Tzu

A silent mind is a non-violent mind —
a mind at peace with itself.

Foreword

There are precious few books written in ordinary language and without the freight of cliché that broker the Being of Silent Awareness. This book is one of them. Writing in elegant prose, Cynthia Overweg is a trustworthy docent in the adventure of great silence. She begins with ordinary experiences of quiet and stillness. Then lures us deeper, taking us to the very mystic threshold where words begin to fray. In a world of tumult and noise, she dares us to leap over the edge, to let the healing fabric of Silence catch us and swaddle our soul. In simple and lucid steps, her words map a silent field beyond the logic of time. Here a river of quiet connection flows – where every past fracture is newly knitted into a future wholeness that has never been before.

The pages of the book are artfully designed and beautifully illustrated, visually creating an ambiance that facilitates deeper contemplation. The text is divided into user-friendly sections, punctuated by pauses for personal inquiry and introspection, making this book an ideal resource for group discussions, and meditation circle conversations.

Silent Awareness invites us on a quest, to an epiphany not of place or person, but of a luminous, still, Being. We caravan by story, taking heart from the shared spiritual guidance of many sage seekers and from the author's own experience and insight. Illustrative wisdom from every major spiritual lineage is offered, and we are asked intrepid questions: each quote and query a portal into an inner landscape of rich reflection on Silence. We will return from such pilgrimage awake, wiser, and aware. Promptly, a dozen friends come to mind to invite along. I know I will stock this volume as a "must read" in our Christine Center bookstore.

— **Gabriele Uhlein, OSF, PhD,** author of *Meditations with Hildegard of Bingen* and Artist-in-Residence, the Christine Center, Willard, Wisconsin.

Introduction: The Revelation of Silence

"In total silence the mind comes upon the eternal."

J. Krishnamurti

There is a Silence that predates time. It was there before you were born and will be there when you die. The Buddha is said to have called it "empty space, the home of the awakened mind." In the Book of Acts, it is the Silence in which "we live and move and have our being." To the mystic, the deepest Silence is the voice of the eternal calling us home to our true Self.

The Silence that awakens us to our true nature has also been referred to as Silent Awareness, the Eternal, God, Buddha Mind, Christ Consciousness, Universal Consciousness, Sacred or Holy Silence, Presence, Unconditioned Love, the Self, or the Unknown. But no matter how valiant our efforts may be to pin a label on it, words can only point to it. Silence just *is*.

We give names to the "Is-ness" of this perennial mystery because we depend on language and image in order to communicate with each other, but words can only suggest the inexpressible. And so this profound enigma is referred to in this book as Silent Awareness or Silence — both terms are used interchangeably, and they are capitalized when referring to the dimension of being that is timeless.

The mystery of Silent Awareness transcends all religions and all spiritual organizations. It cannot be purchased, sold, or given away. It may come and go in a flash or linger for a while. There are no rules governing its availability, duration or frequency. No set path or technique will get it for you because it's not a thing you acquire like a new pair of shoes. This powerful and healing Silence has been within you and around you all along. *You are in it, and it is in you.* Yet with rare exceptions, it goes unnoticed. Why? What stands in the way of the awareness of your innermost being?

Mystics and sages have said for centuries it is our own conflicted mind that veils the Silence that is beyond time. In unveiling this hidden Presence, conflict and sorrow disappear. But the question is, and always has been, what is required of us if we truly wish to break free? What is offered here draws from the wellspring of perennial wisdom passed down to us by mystics and sages from around the world. I also draw from discoveries made during two decades as a retreat facilitator and my own lifelong inquiry.

My aim is fourfold: to bring attention to the Silent Awareness in which we are whole; to suggest ways of recognizing its Presence by learning to listen and see with a quiet mind; to make this as straightforward as possible; and to offer a transformative message in our age of accelerating upheaval. Suggestions to relax body and mind are also included because relaxation opens the gate to inner quietude. The beauty of a truly quiet mind is that it is a non-violent mind — a mind at peace with itself.

Throughout the book, relaxing into stillness is emphasized, along with our innate capacity for wholeness and loving kindness. In practical and artful ways, the intention is to move closer to what the Buddha called "the other shore" and what the Christ referred to as "the kingdom of heaven." We can only glimpse this dimension of being when we are inwardly silent. This is not an academic pursuit — it is a direct experience that opens the mind and heart to the great Silence that sets us free from the entanglements of mind-made conflicts and unhappiness.

Hidden within us is the awareness of our original wholeness — of our timeless connection with each other and the natural world. Uncovering our intrinsic wholeness brings meaning, purpose and beauty into everyday living. We literally see the world through a completely different lens, as if a heavy curtain has been lifted from our eyes.

This can occur in a flash of insight when the mind is very still, but it is also a gradual process of unravelling the conditioning that prevents us from having a mind at peace with itself. A peaceful mind silently sees through the illusion of "other" and when there is no other, there is compassion for the totality of life, for oneself and for the Earth.

Seeing and listening with a quiet mind transforms us. We are given a glimpse of the timeless and silent mystery of our own true nature. And then the endless search for outer fulfillment is finally over.

Sri Nisargadatta Maharaj expressed it this way:
"When the shadow is seen to be a shadow only, you stop following it. You turn round and discover the sun which was there all the time — behind your back!"[1]

1

The Awareness of Silent Awareness

*"I have always loved the desert. You see nothing. You hear nothing.
And yet something shines; something sings in that silence."*

Antoine de Saint-Exupéry

The first impression we have of sacred Silence often occurs in the grandeur of nature. It happens spontaneously when the mind goes quiet in the endless emptiness of the desert; at the beach as the sun sinks below the horizon and appears swallowed by the sea; or when hiking in the mountains and coming upon a giant, ancient sequoia that stood on the Earth at the same time as the Christ or the Buddha.

There is something magical about sequoias. I was introduced to them many years ago at Sequoia National Park in California. The sequoias there are among the oldest and tallest trees on the planet. When I looked up at these serene giants of the natural world, I felt very small, not only in size, but in every other way. Their towering presence felt holy. Their majestic crowns rose so high above me, they seemed to float in space. Whatever I was thinking before seeing them had vanished; the mind was quiet and attentive. These rare old growth sequoias are wise elders of the Earth and transmit a silent and a restorative secret to us.

In the stillness of nature, the mind can be cleared of its noisy content, and then for a few seconds, there is enough inner silence to be in union with the incredible beauty and tranquility of what is seen. It's so beautiful it takes the breath away, and perhaps it even moves you to tears. A truly quiet mind opens the heart. What is witnessed in such silent moments is a resonance with the spiritual beauty at the center of your being.

Without realizing it, you are gazing into your own inner light — the light of Silent Awareness — you are *that.*

Making friends with a quiet mind — a mind that is not overwhelmed with the noise of thought — is what opens space for the Presence of Silence to arise. In my own experience, this begins with letting go of anxiety and giving attention to your own well-being. We'll explore the importance of attention and relaxation in later chapters because they make a more subtle inner awareness possible.

The awareness that is utterly silent may leave an impression that defies description. It may be sensed as a palpable field of vibration that is both completely still and yet vibrantly alive. It has also been described as a spaciousness that is both empty and full, and within it the matrix of life is loving and whole. To live in this boundless awareness, untethered from the suffering we inflict on ourselves and others, is the secret of mystics and sages. But it is only a "secret" because we don't give attention to being inwardly silent. Sufi mystic and poet, Jalal al-Din Rumi, expressed it this way: "There is a voice that does not use words. Listen."

Listening and seeing with an inner perception that transcends the ordinary mind is not common for most of us, but neither is it the exclusive domain of mystics and sages. To live in the interconnected wholeness of Silent Awareness is available to all. The beloved Trappist monk, Thomas Merton, referred to it as "the hidden ground of love for which there is no explanation."[2] Philosopher and theologian, Paul Tillich, called it "the ground of being."

About six centuries before Tillich and Merton offered their memorable insights, the great thirteenth century poet, Dante Alighieri, expressed the same inner wisdom in different words. In the final canto of his *Divine Comedy*, Dante describes a unified ground of incomprehensible love at the root of the universe: "...my vision made me one with the Eternal Good... I saw within Its depths how It conceives all things in a single volume bound by Love, of which the universe is the scattered leaves ... I could feel my being turned by the Love that moves the sun and all the stars."[3]

What Dante called the "Eternal Good" corresponds to what is referred to as Brahman in the Vedas, the ancient sacred texts of India. Brahman can be described as the originating, absolute reality or the eternal loving awareness that pervades the universe and from which all creation arises. It is the unseen substance of all existence, as well as its foundation. In the Abrahamic traditions, it is the infinite Presence of God, Yahweh and Allah, but without human attributes since it is infinite and unknowable.

Yet if this infinite and silent Presence is in us and in everything, then why aren't we always aware of it? The answer given by mystics and sages is that we unconsciously sequester ourselves from it because we are locked inside our intellect most of the time. The intellect thinks it *knows* spiritual truth, but it is the heart that *understands* it because it is one with it. It is the interference of thought that prevents us from seeing this inner truth. What we need is to abandon what we think we know. To say it another way, the unitive state of Silent Awareness is not something you can know with your intellect. It is the revelation of the mystery that you are. Waking up to this mystery changes you from the inside out.

Being inwardly available to this timeless, loving awareness opens us to our own wholeness. This can happen to anyone at any time, young or old, when the mind is very quiet and our attention is alert, but relaxed. I learned this at a young age, not because of anything special about me or my circumstances; there was simply a quiet opening for the Presence of Silent Awareness to be revealed. The appearance of this awareness is sometimes the gift of childhood, when the mind and heart are more receptive to the Unknown — that primordial "something" we cannot name, though we name it anyway.

To better understand the nature of timeless awareness and the possibility of transcending the ordinary thinking mind, in my late twenties I began exploring Tibetan Buddhism, Sufism, Hinduism, Zen and contemplative Christianity. I found all of these wisdom teachings to be very helpful and quite similar in their emphasis on compassion and inner stillness. Later in my search I came upon the illumined work of J. Krishnamurti, G.I. Gurdjieff, Ramana Maharshi, Nisargadatta Maharaj and others who embody the nondual approach to spiritual understanding, and that's where I feel most at home. But it was my initial childhood experience of blissful Oneness that prompted an unending curiosity and lifelong inquiry into deeper levels of awareness.

Since this is a book about discovering the Silent Awareness beyond time, I'll attempt to describe my own first encounter with its Presence, but remember that a description of a transcendent experience is not the thing itself — it is a recalling of a vivid and timeless instance of loving unity that is now over, and this dimension of awareness is indescribable to begin with. It simply *is*. It's also important to underscore that the Presence of Silent Awareness has always been our beloved, though unseen, companion. It is equally available to all and as close to us as our breath.

When I was eight years old, our family lived on an island for three years. Our modest house was close to the sea, where I spent countless hours exploring the beach, climbing on large rocks, and swimming in the open ocean; the beach and the sea were my home. The ever-changing panorama of a colorful sky, together with the ceaseless motion of waves, and hundreds of sea birds gliding and spinning in the air, was a source of perpetual wonder to young eyes.

One afternoon I was fishing at the seaside with a new pole my parents had given me for my birthday. I've been a vegetarian most of my adult life, but as a child my parents encouraged me to bring home a fresh catch for dinner, and so once a week it was part of my routine. While standing alone in the water, I felt a tug on the line and began reeling in what looked like a rockfish. Its sleek, reddish-orange body glistened in the sunlight. It fought hard for its life.

Once it was out of the water, I noticed blood on its mouth where the hook had entered. I had seen such things before and it did not seem to matter, but this time I was inwardly touched by its beauty, and a feeling of great tenderness passed through me as it struggled to be free. It was as if I was seeing for the first time that something alive was bleeding on my hook.

Although quite young, I became aware of a great Silence which seemed to arise from nowhere and everywhere — it was within, around and behind me, and permeated everything. Yet it seemed perfectly natural. As this occurred, noise on the beach faded away. The screech of seagulls and the sound of splashing surf receded into the background, and all was silent. At the time, I questioned none of this. It simply happened, and I was in it and of it and whatever it was, it was vast and still, yet also stirring with subtle energy.

It's impossible to describe something so still, and yet not motionless. Within it was the wordless "seeing" that everything in life is interrelated. This included the living being that was in my hands — its life was an expression of the same life that was in me, but there was no "me" who did the seeing. This occurred within the vibratory field of a Silence so peaceful and loving words fail to capture it. I use the phrase "vibratory field" because it is the closest I can come in describing the aliveness of such total stillness. No one was there; just the seeing. This unfolded as one continuous movement that flowed effortlessly from within the awareness of Silence. And then from within that awareness was the movement of returning the fish to the freedom of the sea.

I was much too young to understand any of this. All I knew was that something extraordinary happened, and then it ended. But my way of looking at the world was never the same. What was seen in that moment of grace was that life is an interconnected and inexplicable matrix: nothing is separate, even though it appears to be. Essentially there is only one life: one living Silent Awareness that animates us and all other life forms, and it is made of love.

Afterward my childhood resumed in its usual way, except it was no longer possible for me to take anything from the sea. I became more sensitive to others and to the dignity of other forms of life. From that day forward, Silence has remained with me in the background: sometimes quite strongly, sometimes much less perceptible and distant, yet it is always there. The same Silence is in you, and in everyone, and in everything. It is the primeval awareness that vivifies our breath and all of existence.

We don't have to live a monastic life, or be a sage, mystic or saint in order to be aware of the nameless Silence where there is "a hidden wholeness." This is what the Christ pointed to when he said: "The kingdom of God is within you." His Holiness, the Fourteenth Dalai Lama, said much the same thing: "There is no need for temples; no need for complicated philosophy. Our own brain, our own heart is our temple; the philosophy is kindness."[4]

To heal the cruel divisions that plague humanity and repair the damage that has been done to the Earth, an awakening is needed on a much greater scale. If we can learn to see and listen with a deeper awareness, our relationships with each other and with nature can change significantly. Then it might be possible for a shift in human consciousness to occur that will save us from ourselves. The oppressive weight of perpetual exploitation, poverty and war can finally end in the inner silence of *not knowing*. What the egoic mind thinks it knows about others and the natural world obstructs what unites us. Thomas Merton said it this way: "There is in all visible things an invisible fecundity, a dimmed light... a hidden wholeness."

Waking up to the mystery of Silent Awareness
changes you from the inside out.

2

The Sound of No Thought

*"Since I've learned to be silent, everything has come
so much closer to me."*
Rainer Maria Rilke

We come closer to the inexhaustible beauty of Silence by learning to recognize and embrace what is already ours. In moments of quiet, when your attention effortlessly rests on something beautiful, like a butterfly noiselessly gliding in the air, or the wondrous light in a child's eyes when a rainbow appears, a gentle wave of Silence may touch you and convey a spiritual insight. When this happens, you enter more deeply into yourself. As the mind becomes very quiet, thoughts fade away, similar to the way the last scene of a movie disappears from the screen. In total stillness the sound of no thought emerges.

It may seem strange to say that you can "hear" the sound of no thought, but when the mind is silent, the fullness of awareness negates thought, and thus what is "heard" is not the usual noise of thinking, but something so still that its very stillness is without time; without thought, image, memory or word. Silence has its own sound. When the Presence of this Silence arises, we feel its spaciousness and its sacredness.

The great sage and spiritual teacher, Jiddu Krishnamurti, referred to this Silence as "the immeasurable." His direct experience of total silence is poetically depicted in his journals, where he describes his frequent communion with the natural world. Krishnamurti's respect for nature is a source of inspiration for anyone who loves the beauty of wild places. He spent countless hours hiking in mountains and forests and was deeply attuned to the presence of the unseen. In the following excerpt from *Krishnamurti's Notebook*, he describes a complete surrender to silence on a visit to India:

"Everywhere there was silence; the hills were motionless, the trees were still and the riverbeds empty; the birds had found shelter for the night and everything was still, even the village dogs. It had rained and the clouds were motionless. Silence grew and became intense, wider and deeper. What was outside was now inside; the brain which had listened to the silence of the hills, fields and groves was itself now silent; it no longer listened to itself; it had gone through that and had become quiet, naturally, without any enforcement. It was still ready to stir itself in the instant. It was still, deep within itself; like a bird that folds its wings, it had folded upon itself; it was not asleep or lazy, but in folding upon itself, it had entered into depths which were beyond itself."[5]

On another occasion while hiking near his home in Ojai, California, Krishnamurti was sitting on a rock and noticed how the hot sun had caused it to crack over time. Then, inside the rock's crevices, he saw "dozens of tiny little living things scurrying about and there was that utter silence, complete and infinite."[6]

The Silence that is infinite waits for us to recognize it as our own. A Sufi proverb, attributed to Rumi, says this perfectly: "What you seek is seeking you." And yet there is nothing we can "do" to invite, compel or entreat Silence to arise. In fact, it is by *not doing* and *not striving* that the awareness of Silence occurs. The ambition to achieve a result will not open the inner door to the sacred. This is a mystery that cannot be grasped by the ordinary mind, and ambition only keeps you spinning in circles.

In order to have a meaningful exploration of what veils the sacred Silence referred to by sages and mystics, we can peer into our own mind for clues. It may not be as tantalizing a subject as the vast stillness that unites us with the pulse of the universe, but in uncharted waters it helps to have a compass. While there is no enshrined set of instructions that unveils the beauty and wholeness of Silence, there is one thing in particular that closes us off from its mystery: our addiction to thinking. The thinking mind shuts the door to Silent Awareness with its constant buzz of thoughts, opinions, and judgments. In Buddhism, it is called "monkey mind" because like a monkey, the thinking mind makes an awful lot of noise. This incessant chatter has to cease for a finer quality of awareness to be revealed. Yet thinking is the mind's default position. As Zen philosopher, Alan Watts put it: "Once you've learned to think, you can't stop."

You may already be acquainted with the talking shadows that run riot in the brain-matter between our ears — the intrusive specters of the past that distort or hijack the aliveness of the present moment. They are also the phantoms of future worries that rob us of energy and joy, and make us prisoners of imagined events. Past and future are terrible disrupters of inner silence. Everything that has been drilled into our heads since birth — race, gender, sexuality, religion, education, personal appearance and economic status — all contribute to the noise that obstructs our access to silent equilibrium.

It must also be said that the mind can be a very good friend. We obviously need it to relate with each other and the world. It makes it possible to find a grocery store, play chess, create art, music and poetry, or invent the next technological or medical breakthrough. The human mind can be brilliant. But the flip side is that much of our thinking is rooted primarily in self-interest. Even spiritual communities can be self-serving or tribal. Some may think their spiritual "tribe" is the most enlightened one, or that they "know" something others don't, or their "path" is the right one.

Subservience to the thinking mind is a kind of madness; we might as well be wearing a straitjacket because the ever-talking mind is a self-made prison that stops us from discovering the transcendental nature of our own being. Without inner quietude, the voice of conscience is drowned out by confusion and conflict; by being "right" rather than being kind. If you have observed the subterranean workings of your mind for a while, you know from experience that learning how it works is an ongoing project demanding attention and energy. As both Krishnamurti and Gurdjieff frequently pointed out, most of our thoughts are generated from years of recorded history stored in our brain about ourselves, other people, and the world. Without realizing it, we are deeply identified with a lifetime of memories and the emotional responses they invoke.

You can test this out for yourself. The next time you get angry try to track the anger back to the thought that triggered it. If you can do this, it can lead to an insight that is useful the next time anger arises. But you may not be able to locate the precise thought that fired up the anger because what we identify with is so ingrained and habitual it is rarely even noticed. And once a thought triggers a potent emotion, it moves through the body so fast that an unpleasant reaction is instantaneous. This is what makes it so difficult to break the spell of the thinking egoic mind because unless we are keenly aware of our thought patterns, we automatically *believe* what we think.

Thought-belief cuts off the inner link to silence and causes enormous division in the world. It breaks apart families, marriages and friendships — it starts wars. Many people are so strongly attached to their beliefs they unknowingly identify themselves *as* their beliefs. The result is polarization throughout the world. Millions of people are absolutely convinced that their inner commentary about others, themselves, and their specific worldview is justified and correct. And so it's no surprise that the world is fractured by a tenacious attachment to economic, religious and cultural beliefs that are held to be true, even though others are harmed or even killed by such beliefs.

How can the world change for the better when millions of people live inside a personal and societal belief bubble?

To make friends with the beauty of Silence, a sincere questioning of what we believe is the starting point. But before that can happen, it helps greatly to *notice* and *acknowledge* that most of the time, *we believe our thoughts*. It goes something like this: "I *think* you are an idiot, and therefore you *are* an idiot." Or the same opinion can be directed inwardly: "I said a stupid thing again. I'm an idiot and I'll always be one." Even those who have spent years inquiring into the structure of the egoic mind get trapped in it. But all is not in vain because the instant we recognize that we are *not* our thoughts, and we are *not* the stories and images stored in our brain about past or future, and stop believing them, there is freedom from the tyranny of the talking mind, at least for a while.

What notices this noise in our heads is a bridge to the fullness of Silent Awareness. This inner noticing or self-observation is subtle and powerful because in witnessing ourselves as we are, without praise or blame, we suddenly become *aware of a deeper awareness* that "sees" without the filter of thought — a finer perception seen from within.

Being aware of this subtle quality of inner awareness marks the birth of a new life. Like the mythical bird, the phoenix, that is reborn from the ashes of its former self, this expanded awareness has a skyward view, a vision much bigger than the talking mind. This makes it possible to break free of its grip. A space of quiet appears that was not there before. From that space, the awareness of self-observation arises. We can then watch the mind-made self in action and awaken from what Gurdjieff called "waking sleep" or what Krishnamurti referred to as the "conditioned mind." In the East, it is known as the ignorance that only sees a separate self. Waking up from the illusion of a separate self can be immediate, but for most of us, it is a process of learning to see through the illusion — a paradox that opens more space in the mind for the eventual realization that we are entwined in a mysterious unity that appears as multiplicity.

By opening the mind to at least the possibility that we are not separate from each other, but rather a part of each other's awareness, and that we exist within a greater unknown awareness, spiritual inquiry can be free of external influences. Then it is possible to be comfortable with not knowing what the intellect wants to know and to sit quietly expecting nothing. To expect nothing is not exactly a winning proposition in a world of brutal competition and "me" first ideology. But the awareness that is silent is not in the dimension of time, and so time-driven imperatives are irrelevant.

An insight that flows from Silent Awareness is the ultimate conveyor of wisdom because it is revealed to you directly — it is not the borrowed wisdom of someone else. It's your own. No one can instruct you in how to be what you already are in the deepest part of your being. To be subsumed in Silence is to surrender the sense of a separate self without being told how to do it.

Yet spiritual help is needed along the way and it arrives in many different forms – quite often someone or something shows up in your life at the moment when you need it most. I'll give you an example from my own life: when my mother died of lung cancer some years ago, painful memories of her courageous struggle with the disease drove me into an existential crisis. While I had accepted her death, the pain she endured brought despair. One day I was going through a box of her favorite things and found a bookmark with the following psalm printed on it: "Be still and know that I am God." This had a profound and healing effect. In my experience and perhaps in yours too, in the midst of spiritual turmoil, subtle energies respond, sometimes in the form of finding an unexpected treasure inside a wooden box. The poet, Rainer Maria Rilke, said it elegantly: "In the difficult are the friendly forces, the hands that work on us."

Even the world's greatest sages and saints had help when they needed it. One of the most vivid examples is in the life of the Buddha before he became known as the "Awakened One." You may be familiar with the story, but it's one that needs to be told and retold.

For six years, the future Buddha lived in the forest and followed a very strict ascetic way of life. He denied his body even the basics of an adequate diet, and after years of such deprivation, he had nearly starved himself to death. Like many other spiritual seekers in his day, he believed it would help him reach nirvana, the state of bliss more quickly. He was terribly emaciated and close to death as a result of this belief, when a young woman, named Sujata, offered him a bowl of milk and rice. He gratefully accepted her offer.

As he ate the food, his body strengthened and he realized that mistreating the body would not bring enlightenment. It was a critical turning point in his quest for Self-realization and provided the basis for what was later called the Middle Way. Had Sujata not come along when she did, the starving ascetic who later became the Buddha may have died, and the revolutionary insights of Buddhism might never have been transmitted to us. The story illustrates the danger of blind belief, and demonstrates that a crucial insight, brought about by an encounter with a stranger, can change the course of one's life *if* there is enough inner silence to receive the insight.

When I reflect on the exchange that took place between Sujata and the Buddha, it resonates as a meeting that occurred in mutual silence. The offering of a bowl of rice to a man dying of hunger, and his humble acceptance of the food conveys love. Love arises when we participate in a genuine act of kindness without a motive. People engage in spontaneous acts of kindness all over the world every day and it may be the reason that what we call civilization hasn't yet collapsed after centuries of endless war.

If kindness matters to you, there are two questions to ask yourself: Am I awake to the suffering of others and to my own suffering? Do I see what needs to change in me, if I want a more harmonious world? These questions are a way to probe our own motives and feelings. A famous remark made by Mahatma Gandhi is instructive. In the midst of India's long struggle for independence, a journalist asked him if he would give a message to the world about nonviolence. Because the question was asked on his day of silence, he wrote his answer on a scrap of paper: "My life is my message."

The truth that is captured in his comment reminds us that how we live in the world sends a message to others. Gandhi's words are humbling and they correspond to Krishnamurti's often repeated statement: "You are the world and the world is you." To dwell with this insight is a worthwhile endeavor because if history teaches us anything, it is that our species has not yet come to grips with its horribly destructive tendencies. There are now almost eight billion people on the planet and that number could swell to nearly ten billion in less than three decades.[7] Many millions of them will become climate change refugees because of prolonged drought in some countries, torrential rain and rising sea levels in others.[8]

The old mind-made power structure that damages the Earth and keeps billions of people in poverty has to change if we want our children and grandchildren to live on a healthy and sustainable planet. Technology will not save us from mega-droughts, mass extinction of species, or alleviate the suffering that is already ravaging many parts of the world. A much deeper awareness of the interconnectedness of life is essential, not tomorrow, but *now*. Nothing changes unless we change. Once again I will quote Krishnamurti: "When I understand myself, I understand you, and out of that understanding comes love."[9]

To finally understand ourselves is the clarion call that can bring about a fundamental change — a compassionate and unified mind and heart. Isn't that what we want — to be unified and at peace with ourselves and the world — to be happy? The Dalai Lama says it this way: "I believe that the very purpose of life is to be happy... we should devote our most serious efforts to bringing about mental peace."[10] And of course, peace comes from a silent mind.

In the following chapter, a suggestion is offered to begin our adventure into the awareness that is timeless.

Seeing and listening with a silent mind transforms us,
and it can also transform our world.

3

Being with the Earth
Awareness Suggestion #1

*"Those who contemplate the beauty of the Earth
find reserves of strength that will endure as long as life lasts."*

Rachel Carson

This suggestion is a simple and uplifting way to lose your mind and wake up to the presence of the natural world. We barely notice the everyday wonders of nature, so this is an opportunity to be aware of the Silent Awareness that permeates life.

Make an appointment with yourself to witness the sun rise. Yes, it means getting up before dawn, so envision yourself going on an early morning adventure to a place you have never been before, because no matter how many times you see a sunrise, it's always new, when you are inwardly present. Witnessing the sun rise elevates your morning energy level naturally, without caffeine, and with silence.

Choose a morning when you have no deadline or need to be somewhere else. You are making and keeping this appointment with yourself so that you may understand yourself and others better. In doing so, there is no lusting for a result. You are simply looking into an awareness of yourself and your relationship with nature.

You can view the sun rise in your own backyard, from your apartment, or any place of your choosing. Invite someone to join you if you wish, but once you are at your sunrise rendezvous spot, even if it's at home, agree with each other to stay silent. You have now entered the *silent zone*.

Find a place in the cool predawn air, while the sky is still dark and birds have not yet begun their chant to the dawn. Sit or stand in a place with a good perspective of the horizon. If you are in your backyard or on your apartment balcony, you may not have a vista of the horizon. That's okay. You can experience the stillness of dawn anywhere.

Notice your surroundings and the sky above in absolute silence. Take several deep breaths, inhaling and exhaling slowly. Feel the movement of air as it fills your lungs and leaves again. Be aware of your breath: it connects you to the invisible rhythm of life.

When thoughts appear — and they will — let them come and go, without tension, comment, judgment, or irritation. We can't force our thoughts to stop, so let them appear and disappear like soap bubbles in the air.

Allow a sense of relaxation to fill you. There is nowhere else you have to be, so relax, and be where you are. Relax, let go, and feel the presence of the Earth beneath your feet. Take a moment to notice that the Earth supports your body, whether you stand on the ground, sit on a rock, or in a chair. The Earth is at home with you, and you are at home with the Earth. *You are aware of your awareness of the Earth.* And the Earth is alive to itself. It is the Presence of Silent Awareness that makes all of this possible.

Your awareness of the Earth and your relationship with its beauty occurs because the mind is quiet. When the first rays of light appear in the sky, you are a witness to the rapture of heaven and earth, not "out there" in the cosmos, but within *you*. All of creation is within you. It is not separate from you, even though it appears to be.

As the first luminous rays of morning light reach your eyes, night willingly surrenders to the birth of a new day. There is absolutely no resistance. Night and day flow together as one movement in a continual rhythm of birth and death, which also takes place in you. Your body is constantly replacing old cells with new ones. The cycles in nature are *your* cycles.

As the sky lights up with color, notice the response of your body to the silent art of nature. Breathe in the vibrant energy of the first rays of light. Let this newborn light fill you, just as it fills the sky and the Earth. The talking mind is absent. There is only the magnificence of nature's stunning spectacle. In this state of being, the identity of "me" is gone. Even the concept of time has vanished. There is only the present moment, which is complete and whole within your *awareness* of darkness becoming light.

Your true nature is the light of Silent Awareness.

*We come closer to Silence by learning to recognize
and embrace what is already ours.*

*In witnessing ourselves as we are, without praise or blame,
we are suddenly aware of a deeper awareness.*

*An insight that flows from Silent Awareness is revealed to you
directly — it is not the borrowed wisdom of someone else.
It is your own.*

4

Wisdom of the Heart

"I live my life in widening circles that reach out across the world."
Rainer Maria Rilke

ainer Maria Rilke is someone I turn to when the eloquence of a great poet can add needed perspective to the inner life. He bravely went into the womb of his own inner longing and came out newly born, ripened by the silent wisdom that he said "takes hold of even the smallest thing and pulls it to the heart of the world."[11] He wrote of the "widening circles" of an inner vision in which he rotates around the "primordial tower" for thousands of years. This subtle, soundless and circular "pull" to the "heart of the world" silently calls us to remember our origin in the infinite source of us all. It is a powerful, irresistible mutual attraction of divine and human energies, a magnetic reciprocity beyond the dance of time. But the human dimension of this relationship cannot hear the whisper of this primordial Silence or recognize its unconditioned love when the noisy, fragmented mind dominates our daily life.

The "still point of the turning world," as T.S. Eliot famously expressed it, can only be glimpsed by a spiritual awakening that may turn your life upside down, usually incrementally, or by a blissful visitation of total Silence, which does the same thing.

For Rilke, like most of us, it was a lifelong process that was greatly enhanced by making friends with Silence. His sensitive way of expressing the inexpressible and his candor about his own inner longing came from a wise heart and it made him a wonderful poet.

Like the woven strands of our DNA, the silent mystery that permeates the whole of life is intertwined with the longing of the heart for union with the One, with Divine Love. This longing usually begins tentatively with the same question that has been asked for centuries about the purpose and meaning of life. If the question is sincere, there is feeling in it, maybe even a sense of urgency because we truly care about what the question implies, not only for ourselves, but for the whole of humanity. Questions about suffering, the impermanence of life and our role in the drama and wonder of the universe arise from the center of our being — the heart. The human heart is a vital organ in the body, but it is also an energy center for the inner awareness of unconditioned love. The heart understands this even if we do not.

Known as the heart chakra, it is a vibratory field of love that is said to be both inside and outside the body, and radiates at the center of the chest. Names like "heart chakra," mystical heart, or the internal space of wisdom are given to mysteries we don't fully understand so that we can have a dialogue and share insights. But more importantly, your own experience may tell you that when you feel love and compassion, it is felt inwardly as a vibration, a stirring energy and warmth in or near the heart.

We often ignore the gentle tug of the heart, even forgetting at times that we have a heart. This forgetting is bound up with a lack of sensitivity and our own self-interest. We're all in the same boat when it comes to what is good for "me." Yet the wish to understand where we come from, what we are, and where we're going — the three questions that French artist, Paul Gauguin, made famous in his iconic painting — are recurring questions that have been asked throughout history. They may be daunting and unanswerable, but the inner quest, if it is heartfelt, goes on anyway. We may not realize it at first, but the faint call from within asks us to "lift the veil that obscures the heart, and there you will find what you are looking for," as Kabir Das, the great fifteenth century Indian mystic and poet said. Lifting the veil is not easy of course. A Native American proverb expresses the same challenge in different words: "The longest and most sacred journey you will ever make is from your head to your heart."

If you close your eyes and ask yourself what you'd like to understand about divine or unconditioned love and whether it's possible for you to connect with such love, you may discover a quiet, but unmistakable longing in your heart for a response. You may also sense that this heart-longing is what gives your question its energy. The sincere yearning of the heart is what drives the inner search.

When we are quiet enough or tired enough of old patterns that merely repeat the past, the wisdom of the heart prompts a remembrance of something much greater than the small self. This prompting may be very subtle and go unnoticed without inner attention, so when there seems to be an impasse, it's helpful to stop, be quiet and listen. There is a wondrous Silence inside us that sees our spiritual poverty and our brokenness, and reaches out with invisible hands to offer the fullness of our inherent possibilities.

One of India's greatest sages, Ramana Maharshi, was said to be the very embodiment of Silence. When he spoke, a vibration of silence was transmitted to receptive listeners because what he said did not come from the thinking mind. It came from the wholeness of a great inner silence. The potency of his silence was a gift to people with the sensitivity to recognize his silence as their own. This made him a beloved teacher. Wisdom teachers transmit the indescribable fragrance of Silent Awareness by their presence, which is felt in the receptive heart as unconditioned love or unbounded compassion.

In India's great epic of Self-revelation, the Bhagavad Gita, this transcendent love is conveyed to Arjuna by Lord Krishna when he says: "I am the Silence of the unknown and the wisdom of the wise."[12] What Arjuna learns from Krishna about the ferocious battles that torment his life is the same lesson we must all learn: the outer battles we have with others are reflections of the battles within ourselves. There is no difference between outer and inner conflicts in that sense. In the compassionate heart of the silent and infinite awareness that Krishna represents, conflict disappears in the light of self-transcendence.

When you dip into the illuminative work of self-inquiry and sit quietly expecting nothing, the mind drops its resistance to quietude and surrenders to the longing of the heart for spiritual understanding. "Surrender" is a word that usually falls into the category of weakness or cowardliness, but once again, it is the context that matters. There can be no inner freedom without surrender. The inner journey is itself a surrendering of the old to the possibility of something new. The Christ suggested this when he said:

"If anyone wants to follow me, he must deny himself, pick up his cross, and follow me."[13] He was conveying a perennial truth to the few who would listen: transformation comes at the expense of the person called "me." To "deny" myself is to surrender or sacrifice my smallness to the gravitational pull of something greater, and then it is possible to "rise up rooted, like trees," as Rilke wrote in his superb poem, "Gravity's Law."[14]

Another way of expressing the meaning of surrender can be found in the Mundaka Upanishad, from India's Vedic scriptures:

"Like two birds of golden plumage, inseparable companions, the individual self and the Immortal Self are perched on the branches of the same tree. The individual self, deluded by forgetfulness of his identity with the divine Self, bewildered by his ego, grieves and is sad. But when he recognizes his own true Self, and beholds his glory, he grieves no more."[15]

Piercing insights hungrily devoured through the spiritual power of wisdom literature can bring relief from the maze of confused thinking and distressing emotions that burrow inside us in the midst of confusion or crisis. At other times we may think we have a stable spiritual footing — that we know what we know — and then something disturbing happens and the illusions and divisions of the ordinary mind swoop in to show us how little we really know. We're reminded in various ways that we are not yet awake — we only think we are. But in rare moments of complete inner quiet, the sense of something changeless in us may appear, something unknown waiting to be recognized — the vast silent Presence that breathes our breath and sees through our eyes. We are wide awake when we are aware of *that*. To come home to Silent Awareness is all we need. It's that simple and that radical, but also elusive because the infinite nature of this awareness cannot be grasped by the finite mind, which is contained within the limits of human consciousness.

This is a good place to pause and take a look at the words "consciousness" and "awareness." They often cause confusion because they do not necessarily mean the same thing, even though they are often used interchangeably. For example, "consciousness" is used to describe the unbounded awareness that underpins life; but it is also used when speaking of human consciousness, the conditioned or egoic mind. Thus the meaning of consciousness very much depends on its context. The clearest statement I've found about the distinction between Silent Awareness and consciousness is from Nisargadatta Maharaj:

"Awareness is primordial. There can be no consciousness without awareness, but there can be awareness without consciousness, as in deep sleep. Awareness is absolute, consciousness is relative to its content; consciousness is always of something. Consciousness is partial and changeful; awareness is total, changeless, calm and silent. And it is the common matrix of every experience."[16]

When the mind is silently aware, another dimension of being is available — not through language, image or symbol, but with an inner perception that reveals what cannot be seen with the ordinary mind.

While our physical senses help us interact and survive in the external world, the capacity to perceive the world with a far more subtle awareness is something that comes to us effortlessly when the mind is silent, and in that silence, the heart may awaken to a subtle connectivity with others and with the whole of life.

It's no secret that if we want a fulfilling relationship with life, it is the heart, not the intellect that points the way. In his gentle and stirring book, *The Little Prince*, Antoine de Saint-Exupéry depicts the heart as the seat of true vision: "It is only with the heart that one can see rightly. What is essential is invisible to the eye."[17]

Seeing with the eye of the heart has been spoken of by sages and mystics on every continent and in every era since ancient times. Heart-seeing is the universal expression of compassion the Christ spoke of in the Beatitudes: "Blessed are the merciful, for they will be shown mercy."[18] It is the Buddhist practice of *Mettā*, the giving of loving-kindness to all sentient life; and it is the unity of all beings through love, as Sufi mystic and poet, Rabi'a of Basra, put it: "The real work is in the heart. Wake up your heart!"[19]

A poignant description of waking up the heart is in *The Voice of the Silence* by H.P. Blavatsky.[20] This lyrical book depicts the intense inner struggle one undergoes to be free of self-deceit. The narrative shares similarities with the Bhagavad Gita as well as Mahâyâna Buddhism and the ideal of the Bodhisattva. A bodhisattva is said to be an enlightened being whose compassion is boundless because she or he has transcended the illusion of a separate self. In hearing the cries of a suffering world, a bodhisattva vows to free humanity from the mind-made ignorance that sows division and inflicts suffering, regardless of the sacrifice that must be made. This ideal is embodied by historical figures like the Buddha and the Christ.

In *The Voice of the Silence*, the "voice" is the "Soundless Sound," of unconditioned love. It speaks to the "inner ear" as the Silence out of which the universe burst into existence. This sound is the vibration of eternal love that still echoes through the cosmos, though it is heard only by those with a wise heart; a heart that offers itself without reservation. A reverberation of this timeless echo can be heard within us as the voice of conscience — a gentle resonance that nudges us to be kind and forgiving when we don't want to.

The inner teachings of East and West emphasize the heart as the center of highest wisdom. Ramana Maharshi spoke of it as the spiritual heart, where the Silence of the eternal Self abides. "The Heart is the only Reality. The mind is a transient phase. To remain as one's Self is to enter the Heart."[21]

What sages and mystics have said over and over again is that there is *only the oneness of love* — everything else is an illusion because love is the only thing that does not die. There are many who would disagree, but this is the direct experience of those who see through the inner vision of Silent Awareness. While this may sound mystical from a cultural or religious perspective, there is nothing inherently mystical in meeting the holy Silence that is already within you. It only seems new because this dimension of awareness is dormant within most of us. This subtle and unitary perception is the ultimate miracle that can occur in the human heart.

In rare moments of complete inner quietude,
the sense of something changeless in us may appear,
something unknown waiting to be recognized.

5

The Breath of Attention
Awareness Suggestion #2

"We need silence just as much as we need air."
Thich Nhat Hanh

Attention attracts silence. Let me repeat that in a slightly different way: the quality of your attention determines the quality of your inner awareness. Without attention there is no inner silence. Attention often slips away right at the point when we could encounter a moment of beautiful stillness. Just when it seems that a space of quietude is available, something or someone interrupts, and then there is a reaction, usually of irritation, and that brief respite of quietude evaporates.

If you get interrupted when you're attempting to sit quietly, allow the distraction to be present, without resisting it. It could be as minor as a buzzing fly or as jarring as the siren of a fire engine. Whatever it is, let it be. Reacting with annoyance drains energy, and we need energy for the finer attention that returns us to inner quietude. Visualize energy as an exchange — the more energy you give to attention, the quieter the mind becomes. Giving attention to quietude is your guide to inner peace. Notice the word "giving." In freely giving your attention, nothing is expected in return. It's an act of love when you give your undivided attention to all that you encounter, whether it's a flower or a human being.

What I'm about to suggest can be helpful when you wish to be quiet and need equilibrium. My suggestion is to read the next few paragraphs and then put down the book and try what is described.

Choose a place in your home where you have privacy. If your house is full of people and seldom quiet, find a spot where you can be alone for fifteen minutes. Maybe it's a home office, bedroom, garage, a large closet or even the bathroom. If a bathroom sounds unappealing, consider the co-founder of Scotland's Findhorn Foundation, Eileen Caddy, who lived with her husband and their three children in a small trailer prior to establishing one of the most respected spiritual centers in the world. Their living space was so cramped that she went to a public restroom in her trailer park early every morning when no one was there to have a space for meditative silence. And so the physical location for this suggestion can be anywhere. All that matters is that you have a few minutes of privacy to give your full attention to being inwardly quiet, and in a place where you feel safe and comfortable.

There is one final thing to consider with the following awareness suggestion and all other suggestions in the book: it is not about seeking an experience. Ambition for a result chases silence away. Remove yourself from the jagged hooks of expectation and disappointment, and let go of what you expect to happen or want to happen so that you can simply relax and be still. When Silence comes, it comes effortlessly, like the sun on a cloudy day. The aim of this exercise is to give your attention to being relaxed and inwardly quiet. That's all. Relaxation and quietude are partners in helping us dissolve the content of a self-centered mind, at least temporarily. As you let go of the thinking and grasping aspects of the mind, a space opens for the invisible waves of Silence to gently enfold you.

Sit comfortably in the place you've selected. It can be in a chair, on the floor or on a cushion. Ideally the spine should be straight, but relaxed, not stiff. There is no need to focus on any technique of sitting. Being comfortable and alert is far more important than trying to sit like a yogi. If your body is flexible and you've had experience sitting in such a way, that's fine, but it's not necessary for any of the awareness suggestions in this book. All that is needed is to sit comfortably, relaxed yet attentive, and to be at ease. This is a chance to give a rest to all your worries and concerns.

To open a space for silence, let's begin by bringing your attention into the body. Take a moment right now, as you read this, to notice how the body feels. Are you relaxed or tense? Be in touch with *you*. Breathe in slowly, fill your lungs with air, and then effortlessly let the air return to its source on the exhale. As you continue to read these pages, stay with the movement of your breath. Feel it, watch it, and rest in it. Bring your full attention to this amazing thing we call "breathing." Just *be* with the gentle flow of air as it comes and goes, as your chest rises and falls with your breath.

Take a few moments to again bring attention to your breath. If you can, take long gentle breaths, inhaling and exhaling slowly for ten inhales and exhales. This can be very relaxing.

The simple act of giving attention to the breath is one of the most restful and invigorating ways to contact your own inner aliveness. Being aware of the body's respiration brings a deeper awareness into each moment. As you continue to give relaxed attention to breathing, notice how the body responds. If you watch your breath for a while, you may notice that the *entire body* is breathing, not just the lungs. More oxygen is circulating and subtle energy is in motion from head to toe. Muscles begin to unwind and tension fades away as relaxation deepens. Your body appreciates the gentle rest that accompanies conscious breathing — the intelligence of the body responds to your inner awareness of the breath. This can be soothing and rejuvenating to mind, body and spirit.

Take a moment to acknowledge the body's role in the adventure of your life. Have you ever offered gratitude to your body's own intelligence as you go about your day? Being aware of your body and the way it functions in your sensory experience of the world brings you closer to stillness. Most of us take the body for granted and forget that through it, we are in contact with the endless creativity of life.

Begin your gesture of gratitude for the body with a simple internal "thank-you." Notice how it feels to inwardly say "thank-you." You may observe a peaceful inner response that may surprise you. No matter how critical you are of how the body looks or feels, it's through the body that you have access to the mystery of holy Silence. The body is the conduit of spirit, and the nexus between heaven and earth. To say it in Biblical terms: "Don't you realize that your body is the temple of the Holy Spirit, who lives in you and was given to you by God?"[22] In India's Kena Upanishad, the question is similar: "Who is that Invisible One who sees through my eyes and hears through my ears?"[23]

Being grateful for the body as a vessel of spirit, no matter its age or physical challenges, brings us to the threshold of surrendering to what is. Be grateful for the body that is given to you by taking good care of it. Gratitude is an energy that is immensely healing — gratitude puts body and mind at ease. When the mind is at ease, there is receptivity to silence, without thought getting in the way.

As you sit quietly with your attention on your breath, simultaneously notice the sensation of your feet touching the surface of the floor. When you give this your attention, watch what happens.

The contact of your feet with the floor grounds you to the Earth and helps keep your attention from wandering. Your attention is now on your breath and also on the contact of your feet with the floor. The body is relaxed, the mind is quiet and your attention is on effortless breathing, and on the amazing transporters called "feet."

We rarely notice the way the feet carry us as we walk: the length of the stride, the way they touch the ground as we walk or jog; the vibration of movement from the bottom of the feet into the legs and up to the hips. For the most part, we ignore the pounding our feet take every day. If there is one under-appreciated part of the body, it's our feet! Like most everything else that the body does automatically, the job done by your feet falls well below the radar of our attention. Bringing attention to the sensation of your feet touching the floor brings more awareness into the mind and body.

Every suggestion that is offered here is for that reason – to bring more awareness into the simple activities of life. It is the portal to the great Silence that wants nothing and gives everything.

As you continue to sit quietly, remember to relax, without forcing yourself to give attention. Continue to notice the sensation of your feet on the floor and the gentle flow of breathing. If thoughts crowd in, watch them arrive and depart. In the gaze of your attention, thoughts drop away, and no energy is wasted by running after them. Let them go, and they will disappear. In this way, the quality of your attention is very different because silence is in it.

Attention is a potent energy. You can give it to the inner quietude that brings integration and wholeness, or you can squander your attention in the noise and restlessness of day-to-day life. Discerning this distinction is the key to being receptive to Silent Awareness.

For the next few minutes, sit quietly, giving your attention to breathing and your feet resting on the floor. Stop reading for a moment and give it a try. As you continue, you may notice that your listening is sharper than before. Body awareness may be more vivid. You may be more alert to your surroundings and to the energy moving through you. Breath awareness connects you with the power of attention, and attention quiets the talking mind.

This simple exercise is a way of recognizing that you already have the capacity to be at ease in mind and body by simply giving attention to breath-awareness and the sensation of your feet in contact with the floor. When you do this, your attention is not occupied with thinking, worry or stress. Instead there is inner quietude and relaxation — this opens you to the silent, loving awareness that is always available behind the curtain of the thinking mind.

6

Silence and Listening

"Listening itself is a complete act.
The very act of listening brings its own freedom."
J. Krishnamurti

Listening and inner silence are inextricably linked. The principal gateways to Silent Awareness are opened by listening and seeing, but not in the ordinary way that we experience hearing or sight. The listening that takes you out of the thinking mind is silent because thoughts no longer overshadow you.

This can happen spontaneously in meditative inquiry or in the stillness of nature, but it is also possible to be a conscious vessel for silent listening by being aware of what pushes it away. The next few chapters offer a framework that engages a more subtle quality of listening and seeing. What I'm going to say about listening awareness is offered as a way for you to experiment with a deeper listening and to watch what happens. As always, your own listening is the teacher.

When you are available with your attention, the transformative possibility of coming upon Silent Awareness happens effortlessly. The mystery that listens and sees through you simply appears; "you" are gone. When you truly listen, there is receptivity to subtle currents or frequencies of silence in the inner and outer worlds. You realize that these two worlds are not separate — they only appear to be.

The first thing that must be said is that without our full attention, there is no real listening. Attentive listening does not involve self-interest — you could call it "unselfish listening" because the egoic mind is quiet, which makes it possible to listen from the heart. This heart-listening comes from our innate wholeness and so it is sincere and loving. A beautiful expression of heart-listening is embodied in one of my favorite lines from *The Alchemist*, a novel about the inner quest by Brazilian novelist, Paulo Coelho: "Listen to your heart. It knows all things, because it came from the Soul of the World and it will one day return there."

But is it actually possible to listen from the heart? Where do we begin to find out? Our first tendency is to *try* to listen; to concentrate. But concentration is not listening; it obstructs listening. Let go of ambition, determination, grasping and striving for a result. Listening with attention is *effortless non-doing*. Just simply relax, take a breath and listen. Listening and relaxation complement each other. Relax into the generosity of listening. To actually listen is to be generous.

The easiest place to relax into authentic listening is in nature, away from the noise and coarseness of modern culture. The beauty of the natural world helps us let go of the noise in the head, and drop the ingrained cultural belief that we must *improve* ourselves. Silence and listening have nothing to do with self-improvement. It is simply an honoring of the wholeness that is within us, but is not perceived. Listening in silence can lift the veil that conceals who you really are.

Nature is a patient teacher of effortless listening. The quiet of a meadow or a grassy plain, for example, acts as a mirror in which we see the simplicity of just being, without trying to *become* anything. The mind is peaceful, not striving — we can relax a tense body and let go of emotional turmoil simply by absorbing the quietude of a natural setting. This can occur under a tree, in a canyon or forest, at a lake or the sea. As quietude envelops the mind, the diversity of the natural world is seen as one intricately woven fabric of life, death and rebirth. We experience this when we are aware of the perpetual changing of the seasons: a robust and verdant spring; long sunlit days and sultry nights of summer; blankets of fallen leaves in autumn; frosted winter landscapes, and then the return of spring. We often take it all for granted, barely noticing the pageantry of changing colors or migratory birds flying thousands of miles to mate and raise their young. We're often so occupied with desire, ambition or stress that we don't notice that the rhythms of nature are our rhythms too.

Poets and artists are intuitively aware of the sound of Silence in the natural world. A poet like Mary Oliver, for example, found a sacred Presence in nature's quiet spaces. She wrote: "For me the door to the woods is the door to the temple."[24] Artists like Georgia O'Keeffe transmitted a similar reverence with her magnificent paintings of flowers — to her, a flower was a universe to explore. Composer Antonio Vivaldi depicted the repeating passages of nature in his beloved set of violin concertos, *The Four Seasons*. In each concerto, the voice of nature passes through one season to the next, just as we pass from one season to the next as we grow older. To see that we are included in everything, and that everything is included in us, happens when the mind is still. A Taoist proverb says it this way: "We cannot see our reflection in running water. It is only in still water that we can see."

When there is attention, we can see the arc of our lives in the rising and setting of the sun, or in the motion of the sea as it sends its waves to land, and then brings them back again to its silent depths. The natural world can teach us a great deal about inner awareness when we simply bring our attention to seeing and listening. The silent spaciousness of the desert, for example, summons us inward to a deeper listening. The song of a cicada is sometimes the only voice that reaches you in the vastness of the desert, until you become aware of the faint whisper of sand moving beneath the belly of a sauntering lizard. Whispering sand deepens the silence.

The act of attentive listening is one of the most fascinating discoveries you can make. To listen this way awakens you to the wonder of your own life. You can witness and participate in the dance of life without clinging to it or making a story out of it. When you listen with your full attention, you may be surprised by the joy it brings once the mind is emptied of anxiety and restlessness.

There are subtleties in the awareness of listening, just as there are many shades of color in desert sand. What is discerned in authentic listening is linked to the quality of our attention. To help us approach what I call "awareness listening," I offer the following distinctions which are not to be taken as absolutes. Your own experience may yield something else. I draw listening distinctions only to illuminate the quality of listening that occurs with and without inner silence. This is merely a way of using language to help explore the beauty of listening with a deeper awareness.

It's helpful to understand why we *don't* listen before approaching a deeper listening that is heard with loving sensitivity. In this regard, it can be said that there are three aspects of listening: *Passive Listening, Alert Listening,* and *Heart Listening*, which are explored in the next chapter.

But remember, these are merely words to help illustrate subtler qualities or dimensions of listening. I've also included meditative suggestions that can help deepen your listening awareness. And it's important to acknowledge that when the mind is completely silent, there is only *one* listening, and there is no "me" listening — there is only the listening of Silent Awareness.

7

Passive, Alert and Heart Listening

"There was a brief silence. I think I heard snow falling."
Erich Segal

Passive Listening

In the fullness of listening, Silent Awareness pervades the whole being. It is a boundless listening that happens effortlessly because no one is doing it – the mind is emptied of itself. But of course this dimension of listening is not available if the mind is occupied with thought and our attention is scattered. We hear the external world with our ears, but with a distracted or conflicted mind. It's superficial listening. We listen superficially most of the time — it's the automatic response of our sensory biology. It's not the deep listening that occurs with a quiet mind, and that's why I call it passive or automatic listening.

When the spoken word or sounds in our environment enter our ears, we are usually absorbed in thought and asleep to a hidden joy. In this sense, we are passive listeners most of the time. For example, when we are engaged in an outdoor activity, we're usually preoccupied with thinking, and so the delicate chirping of a sparrow in a tree barely registers in our awareness, if we hear it at all. We miss an opportunity to stop and listen to one of nature's blissful songs.

The Presence of Silence is in a bird's song, but in the hypnosis of thought, there is no awareness of it. This may seem inconsequential or even ridiculous — after all, what does it matter if you miss the singing of a lone sparrow during your busy day?

In Silent Awareness, such a question does not arise. You, the sparrow and the listening occur as one motion within the same awareness. The sparrow's song is in you, as much as the song is in the sparrow. Our ordinary mind cannot comprehend the truth of our relationship with a sparrow. A bird's song is a reminder to stop thinking, and just effortlessly *be*. The natural world is full of such reminders – it's nature's gift to us, though we usually ignore it. A peaceful equilibrium can be felt in the body when we listen with attention, and when we don't, thoughts and concerns about yesterday and tomorrow steal the wonder of the moment.

In passive listening, there is very little attention available for the people in our lives who need to be listened to. Perhaps a spouse, child, parent, friend or colleague is speaking to us, even pleading with us, but we seldom *listen to the totality* of what a person is saying, or trying to say. The listening is superficial. We hear only what we want to hear, or brush it off, and tune out.

We are unable to silently listen from the heart because we don't hear the feelings *beneath* the words: the sorrow, the need, or the hidden wish. How can we listen to someone else when we're lost in our thoughts, worries, self-righteousness, judgments, distractions or inner conflicts? There is no blame in this. We just don't know any better. In passive listening there is a running commentary in our heads, and we're not even aware it's happening. Often, we cannot listen because we are bored, anxious, lost in a daydream, or thinking about a response. Few of us really listen. We live and listen from a state of waking sleep — until we wake up. And this waking up to the attention we give to listening must reoccur each time we listen, or we lose attention and fall back to "sleep." In other words, each listening encounter is brand new, if we are aware of it.

Once we realize that most of the time there is only passive listening and that as a result, the fullness of life is unseen and unheard, a shift of awareness can occur and a new attention and energy accompanies our listening. We become mindful and no longer listen merely at the surface of life, but from a current of awareness that brings clarity to what it means to live in the present moment. To say this in the words of Krishnamurti: "To find out what is sacred, the mind must know the total content of itself." And to know the content of your own mind, you must learn how to listen.

Alert Listening

When our attention is scattered, our listening is passive. But when we *notice* our inattention or self-absorption, the quality of our listening instantly changes. It becomes alert. Alert listening has silence in it, and this changes our relationship with the world because the listening is not automatic. *We are aware of the awareness of listening* and in that awareness is the possibility of mutual understanding, something we so rarely encounter.

To even notice that we are usually inattentive listeners is a significant step in embracing more inner quietude, particularly in our relationships with others. When we are aware of the quality of our listening, there is enough inner silence to observe what thoughts say to us, without reacting to them, and at the same time, to listen with more attention to the person speaking to us. It is our *attention* that brings us closer to the sensitive heart-listening of Silent Awareness.

To begin our exploration into alert listening, let us return once again to the wilds of nature because there are many different voices to listen to. Every rock and mountain, every pond and river; the sky and clouds, the sun, moon and stars; the landscape, trees and plants, insects, birds and animals, "speak" to us with sound, color, shape, fragrance, light, and movement. Nature's voice is truly wondrous.

One of my favorite listening places is in the Sonoran desert. When a monsoon drenches the parched landscape, the sweltering desert bursts open with the sounds of new life, and the desert suddenly wakes up. A roadrunner squawks with joy; giant arms of old saguaros embrace the pelting rain like an old friend; cactus flowers bloom in glorious color, if only for a day.

If we listen to the desert as it wakes up to itself, we awaken *with it* and *because* of it. Alert listening temporarily ends the hypnosis of thought, and we are alive in a way we seldom experience.

Once you have listened in this way, the stark difference between passive and alert listening is understood. This is it in a nutshell: alert listening has attention in it — you are aware of the act of listening and fully present to what you hear. Passive listening is our usual everyday automatic listening. There is little or no inner awareness in it; what we hear is filtered through our thinking mind.

For example, when it rains, the mind cannot listen to the pitch and pattern of rainfall or to the screech of a red tailed hawk without *naming* it. There is a name for what is heard, like "rain" or "hawk."

But when there is Silence, nothing has a name. If the mind labels people, wildlife, or anything else, the listening is occurring in the context of thought. With inner quietude, the listening has a very different quality.

Listening with alert attention to the sounds of the natural world helps us recognize the wordless language of Silent Awareness. This is why the natural world can be so healing to a human being.

And nature asks nothing in return. All we need to do is show up, give our attention and *listen* for the sake of listening, not to get a reward. Alert listening is its own reward.

Thought cannot listen to the pitch and pattern of rainfall,
or to the screech of a red tailed hawk, without naming it.

Thought names what it hears.
It says "hawk" or "rain."

In Silent Awareness, nothing has a name.

Until we learn to listen with attention,
we are not hearing anything new.

In the fullness of listening,
we listen on the invisible currents of Silence.

Alert listening ends the hypnosis of thought,
and we are alive in a way we seldom experience

Challenges of Alert Listening

Alert listening is a spiritual endeavor because it teaches us a quality of listening that has inner freedom in it. When we genuinely listen, insights are discerned directly from the listening that add meaning to our lives. The act of alert listening is an inward movement that quiets the mind, and it is the simplest and surest way of learning who and what you are. No matter the inner route you take in your search for spiritual wisdom, *you* are the path, and authentic, alert listening is the guide out of the wilderness of self-interest.

One of the most difficult undertakings in life is to listen to other people, especially when we don't want to. Giving our listening attention to the natural world is easier than listening to human beings because we so quickly get lost in thought by inwardly judging, evaluating, admiring, or condemning them. This is why learning to listen attentively and patiently to the voices of nature is a helpful first step in learning to listen to other people — not just on the surface of a conversation, but with an alert attention that is relaxed.

In giving our listening attention to others, sincerity and curiosity fill the listening, and thus there is less room for thought to intrude. In meeting another human being in alert listening, the voice of conscience has space to shine through the listening. Sometimes no words are even spoken, and yet a deep understanding occurs on a silent frequency that both people have entered without effort and without planning it. It simply happens in the attention of mutual listening. To listen with kindness and patience, without feeling pressed by time, draws us closer to Silence.

We know from experience that listening to others can be fraught with challenges. Whether we agree or disagree with our spouse, partner or friend, or argue with a colleague over a problem to be solved, or attempt to listen to a teenager's rebellious voice, a toddler's screams of defiance, or the gossip of a neighbor — we are constantly confronted with the challenge of listening to others without superimposing our own judgments or opinions. Alert listening asks us to suspend our opinions and judgments entirely.

This kind of listening is challenging because we're asked to let go of self-interest or irritation and listen patiently with a mind that does not react and is not defensive. Out of non-judgmental listening, an authentic exchange between people can take place. The inner silence of alert listening activates a current of mutual receptivity that can be felt inwardly, even if there is a difference of views.

Alert listening brings sincerity to relationships at home, in the workplace and in daily life, and thus reduces stress. So much depends on the quality of your listening attention. Does your listening come from a truthful wish to understand, or do you *pretend* to listen, so that you can stop listening and move on to the next thing? Most of us engage in pretend-listening when we are distracted or uninterested. Being aware of our tendency *not* to listen tells us something important about ourselves — not as a judgment, but as a useful observation about what we include or exclude in our listening.

We gather energy and attention in alert listening. A way of understanding this is to sit quietly and listen to the sound of people talking in an indoor or outdoor space; each voice is distinct and exudes a different tone, which falls on the ear differently; sometimes pleasantly, sometimes not. *Listen* to the conversation, and if you catch yourself judging or commenting, just observe it without trying to change your inner narrative. Being aware of the inner commentary slows or stops its momentum. In noticing what interrupts the flow of attention, alert listening resumes by itself. The energy of this listening is magical.

Another simple approach is to listen to sounds you usually ignore in your own home, like the splash of running water in a sink, the hum of a ceiling fan, or crickets chirping in your backyard at night. We often hear these sounds, but rarely *pause to listen*. Make room for listening throughout your day. Take a moment to appreciate that you have the capacity to listen at all. Gratitude adds depth and beauty to how you listen. The next time you are with someone or out in nature, listen with the alertness of an owl, without tension or expectation. Alert listening brings energy and vitality into your life, and all that is required is your attention.

It is said that when the Buddha gave his first teaching, he went to Deer Park at Sarnath near Varanasi. It's the place where he had spent years as an ascetic, and where deer were often present. As he was about to speak, two deer, a male and a female, walked toward the Buddha, stopped, and then turned their ears to listen to him.

A great deal has been written about the symbolism of the deer, but what is important for our exploration is that listening awareness has more power in it than we realize. The Buddha's first talk was on The Four Noble Truths: the truth of suffering, the truth of the cause of suffering, the truth of ending suffering, and the way to be free of suffering. The presence of the deer, with their ears turned in a listening pose, strongly suggests we should give attention not only to human suffering, but also to the suffering we inflict on animals. The human species has much to answer for in the cruelty inflicted on animals. The deer came to listen to the Buddha because they sensed his compassion for them. There is a profound silent teaching in that.

One of the most effective ways to learn to listen is to be silent together. If you have ever become very still while in the presence of other people, whether in a silent retreat, a meditative gathering, or sitting quietly with a friend or loved one, you understand how precious it is to be in the company of people who appreciate silence. If you have not had this experience, I hope you will one day.

In joining together to quiet the mind – not to force anything or to expect a result – we just sit quietly, relax, and breathe. As thoughts come and go, the mind settles down. As silence deepens, a moment arrives when the atmosphere is so quiet, it is saturated with peace. Simultaneously, the listening is alert, yet relaxed. The collective awareness of this quietude is given by all and shared by all. In this dimension of Silence "everything in life is speaking in spite of its apparent silence," as the esteemed Sufi teacher and author, Hazrat Inayat Khan, said.

Alert listening does not react to noise — it *includes* the noise that enters the space. It may come through a window or from inside the room. Whatever is heard is noticed and then released without resistance. The energy of silence stabilizes the mind. One of the most powerful things about meditative group silence is that it opens a channel to the stillness that resides within each of us, and the silence of one is also the silence of another. And so the silence multiplies. The silence of a group can be powerful and healing. When we are saturated with silence, we respond to a person or a situation from the quietude of deep listening, rather than from irritation, anger, fear, or from some old thought pattern that merely repeats the past, and takes us back to the barren land of confusion and conflict.

What arises from this listening is a truthful and kind response or action that flows naturally because we are *receptive to what is.* Receptivity is the imperceptible link between the quality of our listening and the inner door to holy Silence.

Who is Listening?

In the attention of alert listening, the ordinary mind recedes, and more silence is present. Later, when the silence ends, a question may arise: who is listening? This can lead to the fundamental question that many of us ask ourselves periodically throughout life: "Who am I?" This question is central to the self-inquiry teaching of Ramana Maharshi and to alert, relaxed listening. If you wish to engage in the self-inquiry that Ramana Maharshi taught, please read the pamphlet he wrote entitled: *Who am I?* [25] I'll briefly summarize his approach in my own words, but go to the original source for a deeper exploration.

When you ask the question in self-inquiry, *"Who am I?"* a pause in the ceaseless motion of thinking may occur as you wait for an inner response. At the beginning, the typical answer the mind gives to the question *"Who am I?"* is: "Me" or "I am myself." As you continue to give attention to the question, you may hear other responses that tell you who or what you are — for example, "I'm a mother, a father, a businessman, an artist, a nurse," or some other role you play in life. But are you the job you do, or the role you have as parent, spouse or corporate tycoon? Is that what you are? These are manifestations of the life you live, but they are not the essential "you."

So who are you? You may look in the mirror and think that you are the image you see in the mirror, but is that true? Are you the reflection you see in a mirror? Are you nothing but a body and a brain? You may identify closely with the body and want to preserve it for as long as possible, and so you may be convinced that you are the body. Does the death of the body frighten you? What is it that dies?

If you ask a second question, "To whom do these questions arise?" you may be stumped by the question. But as you continue to quietly ask "Who am I?" the mind turns inward upon itself, and you may soon realize that no answer is forthcoming. All that you hear is the thunderous sound of Silence. And then a remarkable insight may strike like a lightning bolt: the "I" whom you think is you, is itself only a thought! It has only seemed to be you. A revelation unfolds, not as an intellectual theory, but as an inner realization: "I" and "me" are part of an impermanent psychological structure.

Ramana Maharshi's approach to self-inquiry negates the concept of a separate self. When that is understood, the real, timeless "I" or the eternal Self, which he said resides in heart, can be revealed as the mysterious Silent Awareness at the root of everything. The illusion of "me" disintegrates and is seen as the imposter it is.

Thus the ultimate fruition of asking "Who am I?" within the alert listening of self-inquiry is that everything we are *not* drops away, and our true inner nature is discovered, yet its silent mystery remains.

"Who am I?" and "To whom do these thoughts arise?" are questions that gradually unmask the mind-constructed identity we think is real. This happens incrementally, not all at once; although for a rare few, the sense of a separate self disappears quickly, as it did for Ramana Maharshi. He was only sixteen when he underwent a psychological death experience and was overcome by fear. But instead of resisting it, he inquired into his fear, faced it, and discovered the deathless inner being, the Self, which transcends fear and abides in Silence.

In the attention of alert listening we can listen to our thoughts in a new way because there is enough inner silence to question what we have always taken to be real. We listen from an awareness that does not identify with the ordinary thinking mind, and thus we can "see" our own fragmentation. With this revelation, we drop all pretense of thinking we actually "know" who or what we are. It's too big of a mystery to solve with the mind. We see from our listening that we are not inwardly unified; that we drift from thought to thought and from one emotion to another. This listening awareness is also seeing awareness because they occur simultaneously as one movement that draws us closer to Silence. In this process, we learn more about the fictitious self and how it clings tenaciously to its identity.

One by one, the veils that obscure Silent Awareness fall away. This begins with a growing understanding of where our conflicts originate. For example, in the awareness of alert listening, you may hear a highly critical voice in your head that is self-judging or sits in judgment of others: a voice telling you a story that you internalized many years earlier without realizing it, and that you never questioned. But because you are listening with inner awareness, you finally recognize it as a voice that is not actually yours, but that takes the shape of a thought or a pattern of thought you once believed was "you." This "voice" may be father, mother, priest, rabbi, or any other authority figure that had an impact on you and left its imprint.

Without realizing it, we are like sponges absorbing the influences of others. This recognition leads to other discoveries of where so many of our judgments, opinions and self-criticisms come from. A gradual unraveling of the mind-creation called "me" begins; an unmasking of what is false is discovered in the light of alert listening. It takes attention, persistence and courage to finally let go of the mirage we have believed in for so long.

In the deep dive of alert listening and self-inquiry, we may discover other "I" thoughts bound up in the mind, such as the "voice" of gender or racial stereotypes that come from a cultural or religious bias we were exposed to at a young age.

As we continue to grow in awareness, there may be discomfort, disappointment or unpleasant surprises that arise, and we may need the help of others who have engaged in self-inquiry and alert listening longer. Yet there is also tremendous relief in facing the source of inner conflicts because we no longer have to be puppets on a string to our thoughts and the stories we create from them.

Inside the brain and in the cells of our body are a lifetime of stored impressions, images and experiences which are unconsciously reactivated in encounters we have with people, places and things.

These past experiences create memories, and memories give rise to thoughts and images, which activate emotions, and then what follows is a reaction driven by the past. It happens so fast, we don't even notice it. That is why we so often look in the rear-view mirror instead of enjoying the present moment.

To understand ourselves from within alert listening is a wisdom teaching we give to ourselves — we learn to be our own teacher. It's the most important undertaking in our lives because it signals the growth of inner freedom. In alert listening, we have the capacity to hear our thoughts without giving them the power to dominate our actions or our relationships. We can then see for ourselves that we are not any of the roles we play in life; we're not the rollercoaster of emotions that erupt so quickly from thought; and we're not the body, even though we experience the world through it.

In alert listening, we wake up to the unconscious forces that shape us, and that have governed our lives. We become aware of the disguises and distractions of the thinking mind, and can break free of it, at least some of the time.

As the mind grows more silent, you may find yourself effortlessly entering into longer periods of quietude, and when the intimacy of Silence gently enfolds you, the inner state of unconditioned love and peace, what is called bliss, reveals your true nature.

As Ramana Maharshi often said, "Your own Self-Realization is the greatest service you can render to the world."

Heart Listening

Silence has depths, just as the ocean has depths. The deeper you go, the more you let go of what you think you know. When self-surrender is total, every trace of "knowing" has disappeared and the mind is completely silent. Time has ended within the vastness of the Unknown.

This dimension of listening cannot be reduced to language. A silent mind listens with limitless compassion. The best that can be said is that it is similar to the Christ listening to the sorrow of a mother whose child has died, and in the great compassion of his listening heart, the mother's sorrow subsides without a word being spoken. It is the compassion of the Bodhisattva Quan Yin, who hears the cries of a suffering world, and vows to alleviate the suffering of all sentient beings, no matter how long it takes.

There is no individual self in the stillness of Heart-listening and thus no subject-object — no fragmentation whatsoever — there is nothing but an outpouring of giving in the listening. The unconditioned love of Silent Awareness is itself listening: the true Self, the Christ and the Buddha in you. We all have this possibility within us, and there are rare people among us who truly listen with the heart.

The finite mind cannot comprehend this dimension of listening and this way of being. And so nothing more can be said about heart listening other than what has already been said. We can only glimpse its immensity in rare moments when the beauty of Silence fills our being.

But it is not far away and there is nowhere to go to find it. It's just that most of the time, we are not aware of what listens, and so we miss the radiance of a much larger awareness. When the noise of the mind ends, the awareness of heart listening begins.

*When we notice our inattention or self-absorption,
the quality of our listening instantly changes.
It becomes alert.*

*To understand ourselves from within alert listening is a
wisdom teaching we give to ourselves.
We learn to be our own teacher.*

*In listening with attention to the sounds of nature,
we recognize the wordless language of Silent Awareness.
This is why the natural world can be so healing.*

8

Listening to Trees

"Around me the trees stir in their leaves and call out, 'Stay awhile.' "

Mary Oliver

Throughout human history the direct experience of transcendent awareness in the beauty of nature has been central to spiritual awakening. The Buddha awakened after a long meditation under a Bodhi tree; the Christ was spiritually tested for forty days in the emptiness of the desert; and the prophet Elijah, after running in fear for his life, stood quietly on the holy mountain of Mount Sinai and heard the whisper of the "still small voice" of God. The wilderness has always been a place for self-transformation.

In ancient Hindu legend, the verdant forests of the Himalaya were once filled with devout sages who spent their lives meditating under the protective canopies of cedar trees to honor Lord Shiva, the Hindu God of transformation, destroyer of evil, and regenerator of the universe. The cedars were said to have a subtle energy which enhanced the sages' inner silence. And so they were called Deodar trees, derived from the Sanskrit word devadāru, which is translated as "divine tree" or "tree of the gods."

Trees live both above and below the ground, partly visible and partly invisible to human eyes. They are rooted in the Earth, yet reach toward the sky. It's no wonder that throughout the world, trees symbolize the relationship between human beings and the divine.

When I was a child, trees seemed like very tall, friendly, other-worldly beings that were much stronger than me because even fierce winds did not knock them over. And they were fun to climb. Trees, especially sequoias and redwoods, still fill me with wonder.

If you would like to deepen your listening awareness, listen to the language of trees. When you touch them, listen to the eloquence of their soft and hard parts: the solid trunk, cascading leaves in autumn, new buds in spring. Trees sing hallelujahs to the dawn, but we rarely are silent enough to hear them. They speak most directly and clearly to human beings when they sway in a breeze.

You may notice that every tree has a different sound. For example, a willow responds to the wind in a very different way than a eucalyptus or a pine tree. The wind moves more slowly through a large, old-growth oak than it does in other trees of similar size, so the sound generated in an oak is unique to itself. A palm tree sounds a different note than a maple. Every tree makes its own music in its dance with a breeze. The size, shape, and density of a tree's leaves and branches influence what you hear as trees move effortlessly in the wind. To be so effortless is a reminder to let go of what prevents us from being inwardly quiet. Being aware of the movement of trees brings you closer to the inner vibrancy of your own life.

When you listen to their motion, you connect with them inside a deeper awareness. In this quiet and sensitive listening, the life in the tree resonates with the life in you. Your presence and the tree's presence gently interact with each other; a vibration of reciprocity arises, and the relationship between you and the tree is alive in the present moment. You may sense the enormous strength of a tree as you stand beside it — you may even become *aware of its awareness of you.*

There is energy and joy in this silent exchange. And perhaps for the very first time, you may hear the "voice" of a tree as it interacts with your awareness and the invisible wind.

The notion that a tree has a voice may seem silly to some, but for others, it changes everything we think we know about ourselves and our relationship with nature. Whether in a forest, a park or on a city street, trees deserve our respect. They are far more intelligent than we realize. Recent research conducted by foresters and environmentalists has shown that trees are intimately connected with each other below ground through their root systems. In his illuminating book, *The Hidden Life of Trees*, forester and author, Peter Wohlleben, refers to the massive network of root systems below the forest floor as the "wood wide web," which helps us understand the vast interconnectedness of trees and their cooperative relationships with each other. Wohlleben says that trees form family bonds, have a network of friends, and send nourishment to each other. They literally "talk" to each other in a language we don't understand.[26]

To be in their presence, without the interruption of thought, renews us. Poet and novelist, Herman Hesse, summed it up this way: "Trees are sanctuaries; whoever knows how to speak to them, whoever knows how to listen to them, can learn the truth."

*When you listen to the motion of trees, you connect with them
inside a deeper awareness. In this quiet and sensitive
listening, the life in the tree resonates with the life in you.*

Silence and listening are inextricably linked.

*The act of listening is entwined with the
fullness of our attention.*

*To give the whole of your being to listening is an act of love.
What listens with love is the deepest you.*

Listening is a spiritual endeavor.
It teaches us to be aware of the awareness that listens.

Silent listening is heart-listening.

Heart-listening is deeply compassionate listening where there
is no individual self — no fragmentation whatsoever;
nothing but an outpouring of giving.

9

The Silence Between

"The music is not in the notes, but in the silence between."
Wolfgang Amadeus Mozart

Silence and music have an intimate relationship, but unless you are a composer, musician or a very astute listener, you may not be aware of the dynamic synergy between silence and music. As the above statement attributed to Mozart suggests, it is the silence between the notes that brings music to life.

What makes this relevant to our exploration is that the silence between notes in a musical composition is analogous to the brief silence which occurs when the talking mind stops chattering and there is a silent gap before the next thought arises. If we notice it, we momentarily come upon the observation that we can "hear" silence.

Beautiful music can help open the door to silence because our attention is drawn inward by the act of listening. I am referring to music that is so beautiful in its effect on a human being that the music itself seems to come from the holiness of Silence. Such music has been called "sacred" because it resonates with the sacred dimension within us, and we feel it.

The exquisite quality of this type of music helps to reconnect us to our spiritual nature and touches a loving current within us. I've seen this happen time and again when sacred music is played in retreats I've facilitated. It seems to give "permission" to let go of thoughts, relax, and simply be still. This mysterious inner resonance with sacred music can teach us a lot about our relationship with music, inner silence and listening. Perhaps this is a reason why the appreciation of the music of Mozart, Beethoven and Bach, to name just three of the world's great classical composers, has not faded away in the noise of the modern era. The music they composed still transmits a sublime silence to the receptive listener.

Other examples include the music composed by Hildegard of Bingen. Her music conveys a spiritual stillness that quiets the mind. The same can be said of the music of Gurdjieff, whose stirring piano compositions with composer Thomas de Hartmann, nurture the growth of the soul. These are just a few examples of the type of music that can help facilitate inner silence.

Sacred music is nearly universal in its effect of quieting the mind and elevating the spirit. The last movement of Beethoven's Ninth Symphony, *Ode to Joy*, is another example of music that opens us to a finer vibration of connectedness. Also known as the Choral Symphony, it was inspired by the words of German poet, Friedrich Schiller. Beethoven's use of the human voice with an orchestra to depict the joyful unity of humanity was unprecedented in his time. And he was totally deaf when he wrote it. His hearing had been dimming for years and at the age of 45, at the height of his creativity, he could not hear the magnificent music that was flowing through him and onto the page. Yet he had tapped into an ocean of creative Silence that brought forth a symphony that is unrivaled to this day. He essentially wrote a musical prayer for a transformative vision of the human race. His vision, though unrealized, is still alive. "Flash mob" performances of *Ode to Joy* take place in public locations around the world, even in shopping malls. And it is the inspiration for the anthem of the Council of Europe and the European Union.

Beethoven was keenly aware of the effect music can have on a human being when he said: "Music is the mediator between the spiritual and the sensual life." When we listen to sacred music with inner silence, our awareness of silence expands. In other words, our own silence amplifies the silence that underpins the music. This can be healing, calming and rejuvenating. Listening to sacred music conveys our nearness to the divine, even though it seems far away.

Johann Sebastian Bach said his music was not created by him, but *through* him: "I play the notes as they are written, but it is God who makes the music," he said. Hildegard of Bingen made a similar remark about her music: "I am the lyre and harp of God's kindness." Hildegard said she inwardly "heard" the music before she wrote it. It was, she said, given to her from above.

While there may be differing interpretations of what makes music sacred, the one common thread is that sacred music helps us enter into a deeper dimension of silence just by listening to it. Sacred music can be a form of meditation when it draws us closer to an awareness of inner silence. Some of my favorites include the Tibetan flute of Nawang Khechog, the Native American flute of Carlos Nakai, the singing Tibetan bowls of Benjamin Iobst, the voice of Deva Premal, and the voice and music of Chöying Drölma and Steve Tibbetts, to mention only a few.

In listening with attention to a beautiful sound, whether it is the ringing of a Tibetan brass bowl or Claude Debussy's *Claire de lune*, we are attuned to both the sound and the silence underneath it because Silence is the mother of sound. Once the body feels the silent vibration of musical beauty, the thinking mind disappears into the act of alert listening. Thought effortlessly recedes. The point is not to get lost in the music, but to be aware of the silence in it and in you. All that is necessary is to simply relax and listen with relaxed attention.

There is a quality in some music that not only quiets the mind, but also evokes a holistic resonance in the physical body of the listener. I've had the privilege of being in the presence of Tibetan monks, whose meditative chanting, along with their skillful use of the Tibetan bell and dorje, elevated the silence in a group of listeners and in the room itself. There was a palpable silence in the air we all breathed long after the chanting and music ended. I've also been present with musicians who excel at playing brass bowls, the Tibetan flute and other instruments. In the hands of artful and attentive players, these instruments create a vibratory healing stillness that can resonate in the body for hours.

Sacred music has been a vital part of spiritual nourishment for centuries. Every culture has its own unique expression. From Sufi, Tibetan and Native American music, to the didgeridoo, to the harp and violin, to the Indian sitar and tabla, to holy chants in churches and temples, and to the wonders of the human voice — the sound that comes through music "speaks" to our collective wish to be at peace. As writer and philosopher, Aldous Huxley, put it: "After silence that which comes nearest to expressing the inexpressible is music."

The inexpressible relationship between music and silence was made very clear to me when I worked as a photojournalist in the Balkan War. In towns where the war had paused long enough for people to gather briefly in public places, small informal concerts would often appear where it was deemed to be safe. These gatherings were a source of rare joy in the midst of anguish, loss and destruction.

On one occasion, I was invited to a concert in which teenagers would be singing an assortment of classical and contemporary songs. My job was to photograph children of war of all ages, and these kids, like so many others, had undergone unimaginable suffering. Their homes and schools had been destroyed by mortar shells; some had been wounded in the attacks; others lost their parents, siblings or friends; some lived in refugee camps and wore donated clothes. Every teen performing in the concert had experienced the terror of war and yet they still wanted to sing— to see them get up on the stage with such resilience and courage made the war disappear for a while.

When a fourteen-year-old girl with a lovely voice sang *Ave Maria*, many in the audience wept. This evocative and prayerful song, together with the delicate quality of a teenager's voice, reached into our collective yearning to experience something holy in the profanity of war. When she finished singing, silence filled the room. The audience was enveloped in a profound stillness that was grounded in the splendor of what we had just heard. And then suddenly, as if in mutual agreement, a standing ovation erupted, not only for her performance, but for the revelation of beauty in the midst of despair.

A direct experience of transcendent beauty is a form of alchemy: the small self disappears temporarily and an astonishing goodness fills the space. And then it is possible to see there is no need to follow a belief system set out by others, but instead, to find what sages and mystics found for themselves. The sudden apprehension of spiritual beauty can trigger a significant change in the direction of one's life, or it may not. In the daily hustle of our profit-driven culture, the longing for the sacred is usually ignored, unless a personal crisis or death puts it squarely in front of us, where we can't turn away from it.

As understanding of the language of Silence grows, the courage to face the fragility of our existence and the impermanence of life also grows. Dissolving the fortress called "me" means facing the fear of non-relevance in a world that demands relevance, a world which decrees that we must compete to become important or rich. We live in a world interpreted for us by others. But each time the mind rests in silence, our awareness expands and eventually the fortress of the illusory self begins to crumble. And then we finally get out of our own way long enough to see that what we seek never left us — its beauty has always been hidden within us.

Silence is the mother of sound.

Sacred music opens a door to interior silence because our awareness is drawn inward by the act of listening.

If you listen to the brief silence between thoughts, silence expands.

10

Being Aware of Listening

Awareness Suggestion #3

*"Don't ask the mind to confirm what is beyond the mind.
Direct experience is the only valid confirmation."*
Nisargadatta Maharaj

Listening with attention takes you out of the thinking mind and into the present moment. A simple place to begin is to listen to a selection of sacred music: something three to five minutes long to start with. It can be any type of gentle music that conveys tranquility. The aim is to simply listen and be aware of the sensations you feel and how the music affects your body, mind and heart. What do you feel and where do you feel it? Listen quietly to the music, preferably alone, but it can also be in the company of others. Just agree to stay silent until the music ends. When thoughts arise, notice how they distract you and then return to listening. The second you lose attention and move into thought, the quietude ends, but you can return to the quiet act of listening — the entry point to Silence — by listening with attention.

In being *aware of your awareness* of listening to music, both the music and what you notice in your body and mind have far more clarity. This is multi-dimensional listening and can be incredibly calming. There are many other ways to give attention to this alert listening. For example, try giving attention to sounds you often ignore, such as the sound a window makes when you open or close it; or the sound of your door key turning in the lock — not just subliminally hearing it with an absent mind, but actually giving attention to the sound it makes. Small, seemingly insignificant listening moments such as these help strengthen listening awareness.

Another example of alert listening that you can try at home is to turn off your television, radio and all digital devices. This includes your smart phone and anything else that might distract or interrupt you. Just turning off these devices may trigger more attention and heighten the quality of your listening.

Once you've turned off the digital world, find a comfortable place to sit, indoors or outside. If you must keep your phone on, and it rings or vibrates, include the phone noise in your listening awareness, along with your conversation if you answer the call.

Unless it's necessary, it's best if you are not interrupted, but if it happens, make the interruption part of your listening. Nothing is gained by irritation, impatience or disappointment. The aim is to be aware of your own listening awareness, and of what occurs within that awareness, including your own reactions.

If you have a child and unexpectedly have to attend to the child's needs, then include the interaction in your listening as well. The same is true if you have a pet that needs attention. It is the nature of dogs to bark and for cats to "meow." It's what they do naturally; they can't help it. Listening includes all that you hear, without resistance.

Once you are sitting down and comfortable (or standing if you wish), take a moment to observe your surroundings. If you are indoors, notice the shape of the room, the color of paint on the walls, the type of furniture and accessories. Include the entire room in your attention, and any sound in it. *Be* in the room, not in your thoughts. If outdoors, acknowledge your surroundings: the trees, grass, flowers, sky, birds — take in the entire landscape and everything you hear.

Observe the sensations in your body as you listen. And then give your attention to your breath; feel the air enter your nose on the in-breath and as it leaves on the out-breath. Notice the rise and fall of your chest and abdomen as you gently breathe. Most of the time, we don't even realize that we are breathing.

Breath awareness calms the mind and grounds us in the body; it makes it possible to relax into the present moment. Whenever the mind strays into thinking, come back to your breath. Take as much time as you need to slow down and become fully present to your breath. Close your eyes, and *be where you are.*

Allow your body to drop all its tension. Many of us carry tension in the neck, shoulders, abdomen or back – and sometimes all of it at the same time! It's okay. Tension accumulates in the body – it's automatic, and we're usually unaware of it, until we notice a stiff neck or an upset stomach.

Once you notice you are tense, you are already letting go of the tension. Wherever you feel tension, let it go. Release it. You've carried it around long enough. Tension steals valuable energy. Relax and give yourself the freedom to turn inward and be quiet. And now just listen, without making an effort to listen to one specific thing or another; but rather, quietly and effortlessly give attention to the sounds that fill the space you are in. As you continue to listen, you may be surprised to discover soft and subtle sounds in your own home or outdoor environment that you have never noticed before. It may be the sound of distant traffic or perhaps you notice the pinging sound of water dripping from a leaky faucet; maybe you notice the buzzing of a bee, or the squawk of a crow – there are many things you may hear with a new and alert listening awareness.

The more attention you give to listening, the more hidden layers of sound you hear. It's quite a discovery to be newly aware of what was always there, but had gone unheard and unnoticed. For example, when you walk into the kitchen to turn on your coffee machine, notice the way the water drips into the glass carafe, and how the sound changes as the coffee continues to brew. If you are a tea drinker, listen attentively to the siren of steam from a tea kettle and the sizzle of scalding hot water pouring over a tea bag into a cup.

Notice the sounds of making breakfast: the softness of butter or jam being spread on crunchy toast, or the clinking sound of cereal as it falls from the box to a bowl. If you listen in a new way to the ordinary sounds that fill your morning, you will be surprised at how enlivening this can be. Include your housemates and pets by actually *listening* with your full attention to their voices and to the sound and tone of your response. This anchors you in the present moment.

If you sincerely wish to explore the authenticity of listening, make an appointment with yourself to listen with attention five minutes a day for a week. If you forget to keep your listening appointment, just listen with attention when you remember. This is not about effort or stress; it's about listening with more attention, that's all. When you listen with attention, you are drawn inward and you actually conserve energy and have less stress.

What matters is that you explore for yourself the transformation that can occur in your awareness simply by giving your full attention to listening just five minutes a day for a week. It could change your life!

Alert listening teaches us how much of life we ignore as passive listeners. Listening is the secret of learning the mysterious language of Silent Awareness.

Alert listening is the secret of learning the language of Silent Awareness.

11

The Tenderness of Silence
Our journey so far

"Remain aware of yourself and all else will be known."
Ramana Maharshi

When we are inwardly silent, a great tenderness may arise in us and move through us. Just as a ray of sunlight resting on a still lake illuminates its depths, Silent Awareness illuminates our own depths and our own light. Within its loving spaciousness, the whisper of compassion arises in the heart. We then realize for ourselves what mystics and sages have said for centuries. We are the eyes, ears and heart of all creation; we are in it, and it is in us; it is one timeless movement of subtle, yet dynamic energy.

To be given a glimpse of this mystery can alter the course of one's life. Life is seen as an interrelated and interconnected whole, not as separate parts. If you harm another, you harm yourself. Any form of selfishness or cruelty is a wound to your own soul.

Silent Awareness is our bedrock and true home. Each time we are aware of its timeless Presence, we are also aware of the singular life that pours through us — we are *awake*. As our awareness expands, we have more freedom to simply *be*. We see that we don't have to sleepwalk through life like an overwhelmed and hungry tourist on a crowded bus. We need not feel like aliens in a hostile world. We learn to discard the story of "me" and "my life" as the center of the universe.

Having painstakingly stripped away the false, we finally stand on our own two feet, alone, but not lonely. We live in fellowship with others, but are not dependent on anyone's version of the truth. We realize we don't need dogmas, books, institutions and gurus to tell us who we are, and what we must do to find liberation or salvation.

This unmasking of ourselves to ourselves is a long and arduous inner process for most of us. Along the way, the egoic mind, so full of non-stop thought, confusion and condemnation is crucified in the light of inner awareness. Out of this interior struggle, a new human being is born from the ashes of the old self. In my view, this is the meaning of the resurrection in Christianity — the inner work of self-transformation that the Christ implied when he said, "… take up your cross and follow me."[27] He was signaling that our identification with self-interest has to die a conscious death in order for us to be aware of what is timeless and silent within us.

In the deepest sense, we *are* the awareness that is silent, but we have forgotten its Presence within us. And then one day, full of longing and aspiration, we begin the inner pilgrimage to remember what we already are, but which has been veiled by the blinding confusion of our conditioned minds. To see our conditioning can happen in instant, but it is also like a long marathon into a steep and jagged terrain, full of pot holes, missteps and self-deceit. We fall and get up again, often with the help of fellow wisdom seekers. But our faltering steps are just part of the adventure when we realize that the "still point of the turning world" is in us. Then we are midwives to our own death and rebirth.

There is no "you" or "me" in Silent Awareness.

Being aware of your own awareness
is the beginning of self-transformation.

The Silence that we don't know with the ordinary mind
is a subtle quality of awareness in which there is no "other."

The intellect thinks it knows spiritual truth,
but it is the heart that understands it because it is one with it.

12

Silence and Seeing

"It's not what you look at that matters; it's what you see."
Henry David Thoreau

Is there a difference between looking at a person and seeing her or him? How about a mountain or a blade of grass? Is *looking* the same as *seeing*?

In the above quotation, the beloved nineteenth century poet, naturalist and social activist, Henry David Thoreau, suggests there is a distinction between looking and seeing, and that it matters.

Thoreau's background in transcendentalism and his experience of living in a hand-built, rickety, one-room cabin in the woods on Walden Pond gave him a perspective that few of us ever consider: the quality of our attention determines the quality of our seeing.

We can look at a gorgeous sunset and not actually see it because the mind is preoccupied with itself. There may be a parade of thoughts about personal grievances, lost opportunities, victories to be won, and all the meandering dead-end streets the mind knows so well. When attention is focused on "me," we cannot see what is true. As Indian philosopher and author, Sri Aurobindo, so aptly phrased it: "In order to see, you have to stop being in the middle of the picture."

We see the world within the localized framework of our personal history and cultural perspectives. For example, some people see a deer stag in the woods and feel a sense of wonder as they gaze at such wild beauty; others look at the stag's magnificent head with antlers and see a hunting trophy to hang on the wall and show off to friends. In one instance, there is respect for the dignity of wildlife; in the other, the deer is expendable if it brings satisfaction to the ego. In this sense, you are what you see, or what you don't see.

When the egoic mind is not dominant, our interconnected relationship with other life forms can be seen and understood as a relationship that transcends self-gratification. Otherwise we continue to look at the world and all its inhabitants, and *not see* them at all. They are just objects to us.

For the purposes of better understanding how we perceive ourselves, each other and the world, a similar approach will be taken as we did previously with aspects of listening awareness. But I'd like to re-emphasize that these distinctions are merely guides in our exploration of the profound relationship between silence, seeing, and what is seen. It's a way of understanding our innate capacity to be aware of the awareness that usually goes unrecognized.

With this caveat, we can say there are three aspects of seeing-awareness that parallel the aspects of listening awareness already discussed. They are: *Passive Seeing, Alert Seeing, and Silent Seeing,* which are explored in the following chapter. But again, these words are just a way of expressing dimensions of seeing that occur with and without inner quietude. In total Silence, there is only *one* seeing and *one* listening and no one is doing anything. The hearing and the listening, and the seer and the seen are united and outside of time.

13

Passive, Alert and Silent Seeing

"No one can build you the bridge on which you, and only you,
must cross the river of life."

Friedrich Nietzsche

Passive Seeing

How do you see the world? Is there a relationship between you and what you see? Or do you feel indifferent to what you perceive, unless it is someone or something familiar? Does your perception include all that you see, or does it exclude what you don't want to see? Do these questions even arise in your busy day? Most of us don't actually see what we think we see.

The beloved Dominican monk and mystic, Meister Eckhart, often spoke of the seeing that occurs in Silence. He referred to it as "one eye, one seeing, one knowing, one love." This "seeing" is not something we can mandate or control. It is *given* to us and it is also *within* us. To see with inner awareness is to see our true relationship with others and the world. But our usual relationship with the world is primarily transactional, not relational. We see the world and everyone in it as a fractional part of our personal activity in the world. This is *passive seeing*; we look with our physical eyes and see only with our senses. There is so much more to seeing than this.

For example, when we encounter a clerk in a department store we generally see someone who is there to get us what we want in exchange for money. It's a transaction, not a relationship. We bring our kids to school to get an education; we go to work to get a paycheck to pay the bills, whether we like the job or not. We exercise to get fit; we go on vacation to get some relaxation. Everyday life is a transaction, usually with courtesy, but with little authentic relatedness. If we are involved in charitable or spiritual endeavors, we do so to help others, but it also makes us feel good about ourselves and the contribution we think we make to others. Maybe it provides us with a sense of purpose and gives meaning to life, which is understandable, but do we really see our deeper relatedness? Is there a quality of inner relationship that transcends any kind of reward?

If we are uncompromisingly honest, nearly everything we do is about getting satisfaction in one form or another. We live in a transactional world — we get *this* for *that*. Human society is structured in this way; it's not a criticism. But if we wish to understand the complexity of the egoic mind, and how it fools us into a high opinion of ourselves, it's useful to be wide awake to the many subtleties of self-interest, which includes our own good works.

It's very difficult to see through the many veils of the transactional world because we are so conditioned by it. Until we learn to see with more inner silence, the world is seen in the way we've been trained to see it since childhood.

In passive seeing, there is little or no relationship with what is seen; we see only on the surface of life, not with deeper insights. There is no authentic *internal relationship* with what is seen, and no real interest in an inquiry that could reveal the poverty of this kind of seeing. In other words, there is the sensory experience of seeing, but it's only going in one direction: "out there" to an object. There is no attention in it, and thus, there is *no inner awareness in the act of seeing.*

An example is getting into the car in the morning, driving to work or somewhere else, and having almost no recollection of the drive there. You don't remember much of anything you saw on the way. The seeing, the driving, and the listening were automatic. You were "asleep" and didn't realize it. The body went through the motions of getting to your destination, but you were absorbed in yourself — in thought, memory or daydreaming. You were absent, not present. To see only with the senses is to sleepwalk through life.

Once we become aware of how much our lives are consumed by this waking sleep, passive seeing can end. But first, there is the challenge of waking up to not-seeing. As Jesuit priest and author, Anthony de Mello remarked: "The chances that you will wake up are in direct proportion to the amount of truth you can take without running away." And that is where the fault line appears because in passive seeing, we do not see beyond our comfort zone.

Let's say you're walking down the street and see a homeless person a few yards away with a begging cup he offers to passersby. Some of us will cross the street to avoid him; others will walk quickly past him and avoid eye contact; some will put money in his cup, without acknowledging his existence. A few may acknowledge him in some way, whether or not they give him money. And others may feel discomfort and avoid a homeless person for that reason. Each of us has a different reaction based on our personal history, opinions, judgments or lack of empathy. We can't help it — until compassion, the deepest truth of human potential, embodies us.

I mention homelessness because a few years ago, I was in a run-down part of Los Angeles taking photographs of homeless women for a newspaper story that would bring attention to the perils they face. Sleeping on a street bench or in a cardboard box is a terrible thing for any human being, but for women it is especially risky. As I took photos, a homeless woman who was not being photographed became enraged, yelling and waving her fist at me. She wasn't crazy, drunk or on drugs; she just didn't like what I was doing. Even though I sought permission before taking photos, she did not want a photographer around at all, or she needed to have more trust in me first. Despite my good intentions, from her point of view, I had violated her private space. That encounter gave me deeper insight into the complexities of homelessness and taught me to be more sensitive.

So how do you look at a homeless person when you see one on the street? Do you really *see* a person who lives this way? Do you even *want to see* what you see? Don't we often turn away because homeless people make us feel uncomfortable, and we would rather *not* look at them, so that we don't have to feel what we feel?

Inwardly seeing our discomfort without escaping from it takes courage. It helps to have the curiosity of self-inquiry in order to approach the truth about ourselves and the world and not be burdened by it. In seeing beneath the surface of what we look at, there is the clarity of inner silence in it. You are aware of much more than yourself and inwardly available to respond with kindness. In this dimension of seeing, there can be an empathetic response.

Without the sensitivity of this seeing, you toss some money into the begging cup of a homeless person and it's merely a transaction; something we do to make us feel better or to ease our discomfort. It is passive seeing, rather than a compassionate seeing which connects us to our mutual vulnerabilities as human beings.

Passive seeing is the reason we have no inner or outer peace. It's why the world is divided and in perpetual conflict. But passive seeing can be transformed into the inner seeing that changes everything.

How do you see the world? Is there a relationship between
you and what you see? To see with inner awareness is to see
our true relationship with others and the natural world.

Alert Seeing

Imagine for a moment that you are on a hike in the wilderness, and when you return to your campsite, you see a grizzly bear asleep in your disheveled tent. The bear ransacked the place looking for food, ate a bag of cookies and settled in for a nap. Even though adrenalin rushes through your veins, you are alert and still. Your attention is absolutely on fire. You slowly tiptoe back into the woods, careful not to disturb the sleeping giant, and find safety at a ranger station or wherever you can. In the urgency of the moment, you are the epitome of *alert seeing*, as well as foolish for leaving food around in a backcountry inhabited by bears. The point of the example is that alert seeing has the energy of heightened attention in it. The sensory experience of seeing the world is not passive; there is alert comprehension in the act of seeing.

The above example is a way of understanding that alert seeing has a quality of attention that can be both quiet and alert when the thinking mind is dormant. But alert seeing is much more than what can happen in an emergency. It also involves self-observation — the awareness of your inner relationship with what you see.

Let's consider an example that most of us have encountered at some point in our lives: suppose you are visiting a loved one or a friend in the hospital. Even preparing to visit a hospital can fill us with concern or anxiety because most of us don't enjoy being in a hospital, even as a visitor. Seeing someone we care about in a vulnerable or life-threatening situation can fill us with sorrow, dread and other difficult emotions. Before you enter the hospital room, if you take a moment to breathe deeply and sense your feet on the floor, you ground yourself in the body, rather than inside an anxious mind.

You can then *observe* the instantaneous connection between thought and feeling, and thus recognize that your emotions are driven by your thoughts. You literally *see* what the thinking mind is doing.

99

This inner observation makes it possible to slow down in a stressful situation and be present for someone who needs the fullness of your attention. Even though you may inwardly feel a range of emotions, they don't necessarily overwhelm you because there is more space for silence to circulate within you. You can then be an authentic source of strength and caring when you're needed most.

Alert seeing is tri-directional: you are aware of what you see; aware of what happens within you as you look, and at the same time, you are aware of both your inner and outer response to what you see. An awful lot is going on and this can happen in a fraction of a second. The awareness in this seeing has far more complexity than passive seeing because there is less attachment to self-interest and more compassion for others. We take responsibility for what we think and feel because we can perceive our own role in the interaction, whether it is with a person, an animal or anything else. We *see* differently — it's inner seeing — the kind of seeing that transforms us.

As the awareness of alert seeing grows, there is more gentleness with others because we see ourselves in them, even in people we don't know. This starts with the realization that we all live in a mind-made box of preconceptions — the world we see and experience was shaped and defined for us long ago by our parents and grandparents; by religious and cultural traditions; inherited attitudes and prejudices about gender, race, and sexual orientation; and by our individual and societal history, all of which is stored in our memory, and from which we respond to others.

We also realize that as children, we took on the role we thought was ours, just as our parents did, and their parents before them, as multitudes of others have done for centuries. There is the additional recognition that the way we see the world is also determined by the ruling government's ideology; by the educational system in schools; by state-owned and corporate media; by propaganda and advertising; by economic forces we know nothing about, and by the dominant culture, which marginalizes those without wealth and power.

In alert seeing, we question the validity of our way of seeing the world because we realize how deeply conditioned we are, and how ingrained our thinking patterns have become. The deeper we look, hidden prejudices and hypocrisy reveal themselves, and if we're strong enough, we don't turn away from what we see in ourselves, even though we may not want to see it. Instead, we bear the discomfort of witnessing our insensitivity, jealousy, arrogance, anger or stubbornness in the light of our growing capacity to "see" ourselves as we are. And we do not blame ourselves for what is seen.

We may be stung by remorse because of our unkind behavior, but in *seeing* it, we can be free of it, and for that we are grateful. We apologize to those we hurt, realizing that everyone is wounded in one way or another and that adding to the world's suffering is just not acceptable anymore. We see that we all want the same thing: we want to be happy, and yet we don't understand what happiness is. And so something is learned that is crucial to spiritual unfoldment.

Gradually we transcend the transactional world of self-interest, and begin to perceive that everything in the world is interdependent and entwined in a transcendent mystery, which can be sensed but not grasped. And while we are not totally free of self-interest, there is a new awareness of our selfish, ambitious or insensitive tendencies. Because of that awareness, we see how the egoic mind creates conflict and division. In seeing this, we are changed from within.

Although far from perfect, we have begun to uncover the conditioning that stifles relationships, chokes creativity and dulls our capacity for joyful spontaneity. There is a clearer understanding of how the past can be a tyrant that dominates the present moment. This is not intellectual — it goes deep into our being and it is the beginning of real freedom. With this budding freedom, it becomes apparent that most human beings are trapped inside self-deceptions and belief systems that cause them and others immense suffering. And perhaps for the first time in our lives, we see the truth of the human crisis. When this truth is seen the heart opens in a way it never has before;

we stop judging others because we see the same shortcomings and failings in ourselves, and so we perceive the world in a totally different way: *We see that we create the world we see.*

We then begin to understand the power of forgiveness in the way the Christ pointed to it, when dying in agony on the cross, he said: "Forgive them Father, for they know not what they do." This statement is arguably the most compassionate in all of spiritual literature — unfathomable in its implications of what it means to be a fully realized human being. To even glimpse the radiance of such a great heart, we are like toddlers taking a first tiny step. And that first step is alert seeing.

In the awareness of alert seeing we are opened to the subtle currents of compassion because we are consciously *receptive*. Nothing is discarded because it doesn't fit a preconceived notion of how the world should or should not be. We accept the diversity and dignity of human and non-human life — everything is included in the great epic of life as we understand it: joy and sadness; suffering and healing; compassion and cruelty; passion and indifference; life and death. We may not like what we see, but we do not refuse to see it.

There is a clear understanding that the mind is divided, not merely because this is discussed in meetings or in books, but because there is a direct experience of seeing the division within ourselves through self-inquiry and moments of silence. We still get lost in our own inner noise and fall back into the hypnosis of everyday life, but when the larger awareness is remembered, alert seeing returns. Alert seeing is effortless. It's nothing that we "do." It happens with the help of attention. You look at a mountain and see its magnificent beauty *without* inner comment, or you gaze into a child's twinkling eyes and see her happy innocence in the aliveness of the present moment, where there is no past or future. When we perceive in this way, we understand that we are an unfinished species with a loving potential beyond anything we can imagine. And in perceiving this, we experience our own intrinsic wholeness.

Silent Seeing

*"There is a huge silence inside each of us that beckons us into itself,
and the recovery of our own silence can begin to teach us
the language of heaven."*

Meister Eckhart

A quiet night in the wilderness can bring much needed perspective and relaxation. In a slower, stress-free environment, the mind lets go. Our attention to the wonder of a starlit sky brings a deeper awareness of silence that gently settles into the body. Letting go and being silent is a gift that has no equal.

Sometimes the Presence of the great Silence we long for emerges from around, above and below us, to the right and left, as the heart embraces the sacred night. And quite suddenly, we may begin to understand "the language of heaven," as Meister Eckhart suggested over seven hundred years ago. He described what he saw in the ocean of Silent Awareness this way: "The eye with which I see God is the same eye with which God sees me."

The transcendent beauty that we cannot see with physical eyes is very close to us when we are completely silent. "It is only the quiet mind that sees," as Krishnamurti expressed it. Even though I've made some distinctions about dimensions of seeing based on how attentive we are, I'd like to re-emphasize that when the mind is free of thought, there is only one silent seeing because there is no "me" that obscures the perception. A truly silent mind recognizes the awareness in every creature as its own awareness in a different form — that dimension of awareness is unconditioned love itself. This cannot be understood by the intellect, but it can be glimpsed when the mind is still. Silent seeing is the total surrender of the self to the Self, God, the Unknown, or whatever name we give to what cannot be named.

Mystics like Meister Eckhart and Hildegard of Bingen have said that sacred Silence brings the universe into the heart. "The music of heaven is in all things," Hildegard said. In her worldview, creation is alive with divine Presence: a flower, a bird, a tree, a human being, each play a particular musical note in an elegant and endless divine symphony. Hildegard's mystical insights revealed a spiritual universe in which everything is related to everything else and shares a portion of divinity. Her vision is the central theme of mysticism in every tradition, and a vision of unity that is beyond the traditions.

This interrelatedness of everything is expressed in Buddhism and Hinduism in the metaphor of Indra's net of jewels: an infinite web of connections depicting the entire universe as an interdependent whole. Nothing is separate; each jewel is a reflection of the other, and of the entire web. To see this grand and holistic vision of creation requires a mind free of all boundaries.

When we look up at the stars on a moonless night, in a place where city lights do not obscure the night sky, billions of stars seem to call us to a greater vision of ourselves. It's as if the starry night sky knows something about us that we don't know. And perhaps they do. The stars are not only above us, they are literally *inside* us.

From what cosmologists call the "big bang" more than thirteen billion years ago, the building blocks of the universe burst forth. Solar systems, planets and stars were born. Those same building blocks are in the human body. Hydrogen, carbon, oxygen and other primordial elements that are in our blood, bones and teeth were created at the origin of the universe and from exploding stars which formed soon after. "We are made of "star stuff," astronomer Carl Sagan famously said. Perhaps when we look at the stars, we inwardly resonate with the mystery that created them, and thus with our own mystery.

What existed before the big bang is of course the unanswerable question. Sages and mystics have pointed to a primeval awareness that preceded all that we see. This eternal Presence is said to give birth to the universe and also exists within it. In India's Upanishads it is said that out of this primeval Silent Awareness the initiating sound of the cosmos burst forth, known as OM or AUM, the primordial humming of the universe that vibrates in all of creation even now. It enlivens everything that ever was, is, and will be. It can be phrased this way: first there was Silence, then sound and then light — the explosion that made the stars, the Earth and eventually the human species. At some unknown time, all returns to primordial Silence.

From the Judeo-Christian perspective, the opening lines of Genesis describe the creation of the universe this way: "In the beginning, God created the heavens and the earth. The earth was without form and void, and darkness was over the face of the deep. And the Spirit of God was hovering over the face of the waters. And God said, 'Let there be light,' and there was light."[28]

A few verses later, the human species is introduced: "…Then the Lord God formed man of dust from the ground, and breathed into his nostrils the breath of life; and man became a living being."[29] The implication is that God or the Unknown Silent Awareness created the visible world from an unexplained reservoir of creativity, and that God's face or Being is reflected in all of creation. To make it even more mysterious, the implication in Genesis is that the breath of God

105

circulates within us. Thus, divine awareness moves through us continuously even though we are unaware of it. To be united with this loving and timeless Presence is every human being's birthright — but we don't give enough attention to our sublime possibilities.

In ancient Hindu cosmology, instead of just one big bang which created the universe, creation is said to be cyclical: the universe appears and disappears in great stretches of unfathomable time, expressed in the metaphor of the Days and Nights of Brahma. It begins in Silence and ends in Silence. The Dalai Lama, who has been in a dialogue with scientists and physicists for more than two decades, has suggested multiple big bangs, not just one, and this seems to correspond with the Hindu view. All that can be said with any certainty is that we cannot know the nature of reality with our conditioned mind. We only know we have something in common with the primordial elements in the stars above us.

Apollo astronaut Edgar Mitchell, the sixth man to walk on the Moon, came upon a new understanding of his relationship with the stars when he was very far from the Earth. When his work on the lunar mission was complete and he could relax and be still, he looked out the window of his lunar module to see our small, beautiful planet in space. And then something unexpected happened. Mitchell experienced "a sense of interconnectedness with the celestial bodies surrounding our spacecraft … its silent authority shook me to the very core."[30] He said he felt a "wonderful quiet" pervading his lunar cabin, and within himself, "an ecstasy of unity." For a sublime moment, he was in silent union with the totality of the cosmos. Mitchell encountered a numinous truth and it transformed his life.

The cosmos is in us, and we are in it. We *are* the seeing that sees this truth. Within this seeing is the fullness of compassion, what Mitchell called the "ecstasy of unity" he felt with everything he saw. Compassion is a reciprocal energy that circulates between the giver and receiver, and even around them, filling the atmosphere with tenderness and love. I've witnessed this loving reciprocity in frontline hospitals between war wounded civilians and those who care for them. To sit at someone's bedside, hold their hand and silently be in communion with him or her is an act of compassion which affects even those who witness it, but are not directly involved.

Throughout history, sages have repeatedly shown us that the way to peace and harmony is to have compassion for others. But we are very slow learners. Division and tribalism are deeply imbedded in the brain. It seems to be the reason every generation of spiritual inquirers on every continent needs to hear the same message of mutual understanding and compassion again and again, told in different voices, languages and in different ways that fit the place and time. The message is not new, but constantly renewed. We are consistently asked to: "Throw away all of your deceptions in which you have walked crookedly, and make a new heart and a new spirit."[31]

If we can "throw away" or transcend the tribalism and divisions that are created by the conditioned mind, we simultaneously remake the world with compassion for each other and all life forms because what divides us is gone. And of course compassion is also the central message of the Buddha and the Christ. Recently the Dalai Lama made a remarkable comment along these lines: "the more compassionate our mind is, the better our brain functions."[32]

This also corresponds to what Krishnamurti often said about the need for a union of mind and heart: "Only the free mind knows what love is." In speaking about compassion, he linked it with what he called the "art of seeing." He said: "Seeing is the only truth. There is nothing else." This may sound startling, but what Krishnamurti was referring to was silently seeing with the eyes of compassion — this is our highest calling. It is also the underlying truth of all spiritual wisdom teachings.

The unconditioned love of Silent Awareness cannot be known by the intellect. It is the revelation of the mystery that you are.

Seeing that we don't see is the beginning of seeing.

A silent mind opens the heart.

14

Seeing a Flower
Awareness Suggestion #4

*"If you take a flower in your hand and really look at it,
it's your world for a moment."*
Georgia O'Keefe

In the following seeing awareness suggestion, one of the smallest beauties on Earth will be our guide to a deeper inner awareness. This is not a practice or technique; all that is necessary is to give your attention to what you see. Notice once again the word "give." As mentioned before, giving attention is an act that quiets the mind and opens the inner gate to a more subtle current of listening and seeing. Once this gate is opened, there is more receptivity for the wholeness of Silent Awareness to flow through you.

Let us begin with envisioning what it might be like if you really looked at a flower with your full and undivided attention.

A flower is one of the most beautiful creations of nature. Flowers bring us joy simply because they exist. They fill the world with color and fragrance. And anyone who has sent or received a bouquet of flowers understands their power to uplift us.

When you give your attention to a flower, whether in your garden or in an open field, what do you notice first? If you look at it effortlessly, without studying it, thinking about it, or evaluating it, what do you see? Can you look at a flower without labeling it, or inwardly commenting about it?

Perhaps the first thing you notice is its color, size and shape. Your mind tells you its name: a daisy, a rose, a lily, or whatever name it has been given. Maybe you smell its fragrance. If you look closer, you may notice the soil it lives in and in which it will die. Its stem, blossoms and leaves form a delicate body that only lasts for a short time. You see its fragile beauty. It may be here today, but gone tomorrow. Perhaps in realizing this lovely flower will soon die, you feel more connected to it, and also to your own life and death. The flower is temporary, and so is your body. Our bodies last for an uncertain number of years, and then disappear. Nothing is permanent, not even the Earth and Sun.

A wildflower, in its tender and unpredictable relationship with nature, lives in the same uncertainty as we do. Yet every season, they return to blossom again. As you gaze at the flower, perhaps a bee lands on its petals to drink its nectar and gather pollen, which helps the flower reproduce. The bee and the flower have a mutually beneficial relationship. And now this is alive in your awareness.

As you continue to look at the flower, thoughts are suspended by your attention to the flower's beauty, or the way it reflects sunlight, or how it sways in a gentle breeze. You notice that it responds to its environment just as you do, only it does so in silence, unseen by human beings — except now, in this moment, you are fully present, and you see its responsiveness: its interaction with the air, the rain, sun, wind, soil, insects, wildlife and human behavior.

A flower lives in the midst of natural and man-made forces that nurture it, but also end its life. In actually *seeing* the truth of this, not with the thinking mind, but from within the awareness of seeing, your own relationship with the flower suddenly becomes more apparent: you are connected to everything the flower is connected to. It just wasn't "seen" before.

In a deeper contact with something you had always taken for granted, a mysterious resonance occurs within you as your attention embraces this delicate flower. You completely open yourself to it, as it has opened itself to you. You may feel affection, even love arise in you. Suddenly a flower is no longer merely an object to use and throw away, like so many other things we carelessly discard. You now see for yourself that even a single flower is part of the grand and mysterious fabric of life. It nurtures bees, hummingbirds, ladybugs, and butterflies. It adds beauty to the landscape; and though its life is brief, a flower conveys a gentle strength to anyone who appreciates its delicate existence. By simply giving your attention to the living stillness of a flower, you become inwardly still yourself. This is actually quite amazing. It is as if nature knows what you need and gives it to you freely. The key is your attention.

In the silence of seeing awareness, it may even be possible to discern with subtle inner vision that a flower has its own vibratory field of aliveness that cannot be comprehended with the ordinary mind. Whether an orchid, a tulip, or a daffodil, the name we give a flower is *not* what it is. We only think we know what a flower is because we assign it a name and set of characteristics. This is what we do with everything in the natural world, until we learn to break the habit of thinking that we *know*.

While we can dissect a flower, look at it under a microscope and categorize its material components, it doesn't tell us what a flower is. A flower is more than its constituent parts, just as we are. We did not create ourselves, the universe or the wildflowers on this planet, so how can we solve the mystery of a flower, let alone the grandness of creation with our finite mind? To see that we don't see is humbling. *To see that we don't see is the beginning of seeing.*

After spending a few silent moments with the beauty of a flower, which is a communion with beauty and silence, you return to the rush of life. But now you have a more subtle quality of awareness. When thoughts appear, you realize they are appearing and disappearing all the time. It is the nature of thought to come and go, arrive and depart. And so you take a deep breath, and rest your mind on the out-breath. You can always come back to the breath to find respite from the thinking mind — remember that conscious breathing negates thought.

Giving attention to just three complete breaths – inhaling and exhaling, and letting the shoulders, neck and the entire body relax into the exhale can do wonders for stress because this quiets the mind.

Breath awareness connects us to the whole of creation and to the timeless Presence at the heart of life.

By simply giving your attention to the living stillness
of a flower, you become inwardly still yourself.

15

The Other Shore

"Those who seek the easy way do not seek the true way."
Dōgen Zenji

In the best sense of the word, what is called the "way" to liberation or salvation in religious traditions is a gradual spiritual blossoming from a state of self-centeredness to a loving way of being in the world. As a flower gradually unfolds its petals in morning light, the light of wisdom and compassion unfolds incrementally in the spiritual insight of non-judgmental self-observation. To put it another way: the search for spiritual truth is an inside job. The authority of dogma is just another detour. The great Zen teacher, Dōgen Zenji, was unsparingly clear about this when counseling those who came to him for guidance: "If you cannot find the truth right where you are, where else do you expect to find it?" Dogen was suggesting the place to look is within.

The road to awakening and inner freedom is lined with the landmines of self-interest. To clearly see that we are in a state of waking sleep much of the time is a process for most of us, but awakening can also happen instantly when the mind is quiet — a quiet mind is receptive to Silent Awareness. Even though a direct experience of Silent Awareness may not last long, what is learned in this dimension of being changes us. Moments like these make it clear that the conditioned mind obscures the hidden Reality within us.

As mentioned earlier, Silent Awareness is not something you *know*; it is the revelation of the mystery that you are. It transcends all religious traditions and spiritual organizations, but does not exclude them either. What is needed for inner transformation is a willingness to surrender the old for the sake of the new. It is a complete letting go of the personal identity that we cling to; a voluntary sacrifice that takes courage. A metaphor for this letting go is a very young bird that has never flown before and must let go of a tree's branch in order to go airborne and fly. The brave flyer falls upward to a new life. For us, the upward movement is of course far more complicated because the structure of the ego-mind, with its fears and conflicts, resists breaking free of its own constraints. And that is why learning to listen and see with inner silence is so helpful, and why it is mentioned in every chapter of this book. Without a finer quality of listening and seeing, we are disconnected from the deepest part of our being.

The mind-made self is like a hall of mirrors at a circus. As you look at your reflection, the convex curves of the mirrors distort your perception of yourself. Your face and body appear elongated, contorted and even grotesque. The only way to see clearly is to walk away from the deceptive mirror. The fact that you *can* walk away is a relief! We can do the same with the discord of the babbling mind by simply observing it — inner silence is the result of seeing the discord.

The harmony of inner silence is described by Shāntideva in *The Way of the Bodhisattva* as being like a "blind man who has found a precious gem inside a heap of dust." This is a wonderful metaphor because it underscores the priceless value of inner seeing. The Mundaka Upanishad describes seeing this inner jewel as the light of the Self at the center of our being: "Bright but hidden, the Self dwells in the heart." We may have flashes of this Self when the conditioned mind subsides, releasing its tenacious authority over our relationship with life. Then mind and heart can open fully to compassion.

This brings us to the compassionate wisdom teachings of the Buddha and the Christ. In different ways, they asked us to let go of what we are *not,* so that we can be what we truly are. They told powerful and transformative stories to help us see our own possibilities. Both of them walked the Earth when verbal storytelling was the primary way of transmitting a wisdom teaching.

In ancient times literacy rates were extremely low all over the world; there was no printing press and no bookstores. Leather-bound, hand-written books were owned and read almost exclusively by the elite and the clergy. In our technological world it is difficult to imagine how ordinary people lived thousands of years ago. If they wanted to understand the mystery of God or the Unknown, they sought the opinions of religious leaders or listened to the parables of wandering prophets and ascetics, who sometimes contradicted what religious authorities said. Very few had the leisure or the freedom to independently explore a spiritual inquiry of their own. It was a very different world and so a wisdom teacher also had to be a storyteller.

The Christ and the Buddha told stories that spoke directly to what it means to see and listen without the interference of the conditioned mind. To illustrate this, I'm going to summarize two beloved stories that share similarities, but also have differences. One story was told by the Buddha, the other by the Christ.

We begin with one of the most cherished stories attributed to the Buddha, known as The Parable of the Raft. It tells the story of a spiritual searcher who wants to be inwardly free, but it requires him to plunge into the Unknown. The story goes like this: a man is stranded on the shore of a very turbulent river where there is agitation, confusion and danger. But on the other shore of the river, there is peace and calm — it is a place that his heart longs for.

The man urgently wants to cross the raging river to get there, but there seems to be no way of reaching the other shore, since there is no bridge or ferry for transport. If he tries to swim, he may drown. Yet at the same time, he sees the danger of staying where he is. He realizes that to reach beyond what limits him he must find a way across the river, so he builds a raft made of logs, vines and branches. And then with great effort and courage, using all his strength and persistence, he slowly and carefully paddles across the ferocious river. Although the river is fierce and the journey is tiring, he makes it to the other shore, and drags the raft onto the beach.

After allowing the story to sink in for a moment, the Buddha then asked his listeners what should be done with the raft now that the other shore has been reached: should the person discard the raft, or keep it? What arises from the responses is that he can leave the raft behind, since it is no longer needed.

The story's meaning can be interpreted in various ways. Here is my way of seeing it: The turbulent river is the thinking or egoic mind, trapped in the chaotic waters of conflict and suffering because the mind divides the world into "me" and "other." The fact that the man sees the difficulty of his situation suggests that he is prepared to make a radical change, so he builds a raft and crosses the raging river, which points to his willingness to sacrifice everything to find truth. The raft also represents the support of the Buddha's teaching, which for Buddhists is the way out of the river of suffering. The difficult journey across the dangerous river also indicates the sustained attention that is necessary to finally see that the turbulent river is not "out there." The turbulence is within *us*.

The Parable of the Raft points to the inner work of gradually stripping away what is false to uncover what is real, a monumental task for most of us, not because it's impossible, but because we stand in our own way, until there is an inner commitment to go the distance to the other shore. The response to the question of what should be done with the raft once the other shore is reached suggests that when the inner transcendent Being has been revealed, the "raft," which is a metaphor for the teaching, can be gratefully acknowledged, but is no longer needed as before. The teaching was merely a pointer that offered help, but is no longer necessary because the voyage across the turbulent river to Self-realization is not an outward journey; it only seems to be. No one is going anywhere. We are the raft, the river *and*

the other shore. In this sense, we cannot be saved by a teaching or a teacher. They may offer guidance, but we must save ourselves from our own self-deceit. The message of the Buddha is that we can learn to see through the haze of self-delusion and beyond the external world of shiny objects. And then we are home without ever going anywhere. The other shore is close, but it is also far away.

The Buddha's teaching about the inner location of the "other shore" has parallels in Christianity. In the Gospel of Luke for example, the Christ says: "The coming of the kingdom of God is not something that can be observed. Nor will people say, 'here it is,' or 'there it is' because the kingdom of God is within you." The "other shore" and "the kingdom of God" are the transcendent Being, the Silent Awareness that lives within each of us.

When the Christ was asked during the Sermon on the Mount why he spoke in parables, he said: "I speak to them in parables because while seeing, they do not see; while hearing, they do not listen, nor do they understand." In other words, the crowds that followed him could not see or hear from a deeper awareness — they were trapped in self-interest. We are not that different from our ancestors. The Christ told stories that place the listener inside the story's narrative to convey a spiritual truth that would otherwise go unseen and unheard. For those who are inwardly quiet enough to listen with attention, something new can be learned by listening to a story that has spiritual depth.

This brings me to the parable of the Good Samaritan, a story that speaks to the polarization of today's world just as much as it did in biblical times. This beloved story is designed to penetrate the walls of the egoic mind so that its message of unity and compassion can be received in the heart. Like the Parable of the Raft, the story of the Good Samaritan points to another dimension of seeing.

The parable begins when an argumentative religious scholar asks the Christ this question: "Who is my neighbor?" The Christ answers by telling a story that illustrates how our behavior toward each other can determine whether a person lives or dies. He tells the scholar and the listening crowd about a man who had been robbed, stripped of his clothing, badly beaten and left to die on the road. (At this early stage of the story, many listeners are already seeing themselves in the role of the injured person, and so from the beginning they are interested in what happens next).

The Christ continues the story by telling the crowd that even though several pious and religious men come across the dying man, no one stops to help him. In fact, they actually cross to the other side of the road to avoid him. No one offers to help. (And now listeners are even more connected to what the man's fate will be. The question in their minds might be: "What if this happened to me?")

The story continues with the introduction of a traveler from Samaria, known as a Samaritan, who comes upon the tragic scene and stops. The Samaritan sees the terrible condition of the battered man and immediately gives assistance. He is the first person to offer help and does so with generosity. He attends to the man's injuries and gives him water and clothing. (As you will later see, the fact that a Samaritan stopped to help is an important point in the parable).

The Samaritan then gently lifts the frail man onto his donkey and travels far out of his way to bring him to an inn, where he can rest and heal. He even pays the innkeeper for the room and all expenses incurred while the man recovers from the near fatal attack. As the crowd takes in the totality of the story, the Christ turns to the religious scholar and asks him which of the traveling men who passed by the dying man acted like a neighbor. The scholar answers that it was the man who showed him mercy. And now not only has the story had a powerful effect on the crowd, the self-righteous religious scholar who posed the question: "Who is my neighbor?" realizes that *anyone* who needs help is your neighbor. The Christ then tells him: "go and do likewise."

To grasp the extraordinary point being made in this parable, it is important to note that in biblical Israel the Samaritans were considered outcasts and enemies, and yet it was an "outcast" who saved the man's life, while the religious men left him to die. The parable clearly illustrates that our tribal view of the "other" is false, and that those we define as enemies may have more compassion than we do. It asks us to see ourselves *as* the other. When that happens, compassion blossoms, and our divisions end. Parables like the Good Samaritan are designed to bypass the intellect and go straight to the heart, where it can be felt as a spiritual truth. The people in the crowd who had the capacity to listen from a more subtle level of awareness could suddenly perceive their own prejudice and their own tendency to ignore the suffering of others. If they were truly receptive to what the Christ was saying, they had to face their prejudice head-on and have compassion for the "other" because the other is also you. This was a radical teaching for its time, and it is no less radical today.

The parable of the Good Samaritan is as valid today as it was more than two thousand years ago. In the words of Martin Luther King: "We are all caught in an inescapable network of mutuality, tied in a single garment of destiny. Whatever affects one directly, affects all indirectly." We are all connected, interrelated and interdependent. The whole of creation is part of us, just as we are part of it. To go beyond violence requires a compassionate understanding of our "mutuality" and our shared wish to be happy.

The Christ and the Buddha lived from the infinite love of Silent Awareness. Even though they lived centuries apart and came from different countries and cultures, their wisdom teachings intersect at the transformative message of inner freedom and compassion for others. For us, the inner work is to bring relaxed attention to alert listening and seeing, and to let go of what we are *not*. This means dropping the absurd pretense of being better than or less than someone else. To listen and see from within inner silence connects us to one another, and builds the bridge that transports us out of the sorrow of the small self to the shore of unconditioned love.

16

The Dark Night

"The endurance of darkness is the preparation for great light."
John of the Cross

As you may have noticed in your own life, the spiritual quest is not linear. Perhaps it can be viewed as a spiral — a gradual turning towards, and then away from the inner silence that heals the divisions of the egoic mind. As the mind becomes quieter, there is equilibrium, until the disruption of the talking mind re-emerges and the outward movement toward the noise of the world resumes. And sometimes just as inner quietude gains momentum, the unpredictability of life crashes in with an experience of sorrow and loss — a loved one dies, or we are faced with our own death, or a disease that alters the quality of life. Something disturbing may happen that causes an existential crisis, temporarily disconnecting us from the inner search or even from life itself.

The form this crisis takes differs for everyone, but a sense of spiritual loneliness or isolation is common. This internal crisis has been called the "dark night" and the "dark night of the soul" because there is a feeling of spiritual barrenness, along with bewildering questions about the meaning and significance of life. Despite its excruciating inner challenges, the dark night can be a wisdom teacher.

The essential lesson the dark night teaches is that by facing our suffering without hiding from it or suppressing it, an awakened

125

understanding of sorrow appears. We realize — not intellectually, but from our heart — that suffering is universal to everyone on the planet, including animals and all beings in the natural world. A deeper sensitivity to the suffering we inflict on others comes into view, and then a life altering insight may arise: loss, sorrow and death can teach us how to live. The experience of loss is often the price we pay for the flowering of compassion and self transcendence.

Conceptually the dark night has been closely identified with mystics who have written about their direct experience of divine union and its inevitable end — when the great Silence of unconditioned love suddenly enfolds the heart, and just as suddenly, disappears. In this context, the dark night is both sublime and austere because inner wisdom is gathered from the passage into darkness.

The visionary sixteenth century Spanish monk and mystic, John of the Cross, spoke eloquently and passionately about his experience of union with and separation from divine love, referring to this ineffable love as the Beloved. In one particularly evocative stanza, he wrote:

> "Oh night that guided me,
> Oh night more lovely than the dawn,
> Oh night that joined Beloved with lover,
> Lover transformed in the Beloved!"[33]

The lover depicted in the poem is of course its author, John of the Cross, and when encircled by the unconditioned love of the Beloved, he is transformed. What is suggested is that the merging of human and divine energies creates the indescribable ecstasy of Oneness, a union that represents the height of human possibility in all the traditions, but it is also beyond them.

Throughout his life John wrote movingly of his intimate relationship with divine love and his poetry can help us understand this transcendent intimacy. It can also help us comprehend its bitter counterpoint: the inevitable pain of separation, which John called the dark night. In one of his most haunting poems, he wrote:

"Where have you hidden, Beloved, and left me moaning?

You fled like the stag after wounding me;

I went out calling you, and you were gone."[34]

The loss of inner union with the Beloved led John of the Cross into the dark night. For someone as sensitive and as devoted to the inner being as John, this separation was a spiritual wound that sliced deeply into his yearning heart and left him in near despair. The dark night can be viewed as sacred grief, a tender and burning longing for a return to divine union. And it has its own way of emptying the egoic self of hidden deceptions — all forms of self-interest must die in the service of something higher.

As expressed in his poetry, the intense longing of John of the Cross is for a return to the unitive state of being. It is what he lived for, and so for him, it was painful to endure the loss of communion with the Beloved. He wrote about this "wounding" with great tenderness. To transcend such a loss, a reconciliation of the twin realities of the human-divine relationship is necessary. John realized that the unitive state of awareness cannot be sustained by human will, and that is the soul's lament. It seems that an experience of divine love lasts only as long as mind and body can remain silent in the Presence of its searing beauty.

John of the Cross, and his mentor and friend, Teresa of Avila, encountered the bliss of the unitive state of being throughout their lives. Their life stories indicate that they both were willing to die a psychological death: to sacrifice the "me" for the boundless love that arises from Silence. A psychological death involves the passing away of the egoic mind structure — the ending of the mind-made "me," at least temporarily. This is expressed as self-transformation in the Vedas — the conscious surrender of the finite self to the eternal Self. An insight expressed by Nisargadatta Maharaj says this beautifully:

"Wisdom is knowing I am nothing. Love is knowing I am everything, and between the two my life moves."

In the Gospel of John, it points to the symbolic meaning of being "born again," not through the womb, but through spirit, or self-transcendence. The Christ said: "Verily, verily I say unto to you, unless a man is born again, he cannot see the kingdom of heaven."[35] Although presented differently, both the Eastern and Western traditions describe self-transformation as an inner death and a rebirth — an internal alchemy that reveals our concealed wholeness. To see the truth of our emptiness and simultaneously see the parallel truth of our inherent fullness is what the dark night points to.

The dark night may involve a voluntary dissolution of the ego, or as much dissolution as one can bear to be free of the self-interest of the transactional world. The biographies and autobiographies of sages and mystics are filled with dark nights that eventually radiate light. For example, Teresa of Avila said she was lost on what she called "a stormy sea" of spiritual aridity for twenty years. During this time she was a sought-after spiritual counselor to others, which only deepened her internal crisis because she felt unworthy of their trust. Her dark night finally ended with a piercing insight that suddenly overwhelmed her as she walked down a hall in her convent and looked at a painting of the Christ.[36]

In the Tibetan Buddhist tradition, the great yogi, Milarepa, went through a long purgation to be free of the tragedy of his youth. He was a boy when his father died and his family's home and wealth were stolen by a greedy uncle, leaving him, his mother and younger sister destitute. His uncle was cruel to his mother, forcing her into poverty. When Milarepa was old enough, he exacted revenge on his relatives, killing some of them. But Milarepa soon felt agonizing remorse and sought redemption and forgiveness. After many years of living an ascetic life, along with the practice of atonement and meditation, he found enlightenment in a cave high in the Himalayas, and then dedicated his life to helping others realize what he discovered in the depths of suffering. Milarepa learned that revenge only perpetuates more violence and suffering — this does not mean we ignore the harmful behavior of others, but that resorting to raw vengeance creates more pain. For Milarepa, this life lesson opened his heart, and in his later years, he became a beloved wisdom teacher.

The dark night has been a rite of passage in all of the traditions. Another example is the great Sufi sage, Rabi'a of Basra. Kidnapped as a child and sold as a slave to a wealthy man and his family, Rabi'a was mistreated for years and forced to work day and night, yet she refused to hate her tormentors. After a long day of hard work, her "owner" saw her kneeling in prayer in his courtyard, her face glowing with spiritual light. After seeing this several times, he set her free. Rabi'a fled into the desert, where she could pursue a deeper search of spiritual understanding. When she returned to Basra years later, she was a source of wisdom and inspiration for many others.

A passage through spiritual darkness sometimes involves a reckoning with one's own life, as it did for Milarepa and Rabi'a of Basra, or it may be provoked by an unavoidable collision with the stark truth of human cruelty and indifference to suffering. In his incomparable book, *Man's Search for Meaning*, Viktor Frankl, a survivor of the Holocaust, wrote: "When we are no longer able to change a situation, we are challenged to change ourselves ... the salvation of man is through love and in love."[37] Frankl's poignant description of his inner life and his encounters with beauty and transcendence, despite the unspeakable horror of the concentration camp, makes his book one of the most significant books ever written.

The search for spiritual understanding is not only an inquiry into our innermost being, for many people it is also a search for meaning in a culture that honors celebrity, wealth and power, while it ignores the noble labor of a waitress, a mechanic or a school teacher. It's obvious we have our priorities upside down. The modern world is dominated by corporate behemoths that exert tremendous power over the everyday life of humanity and the well-being of the planet. The all-consuming profit driven motive has suppressed the basic human need to relate to something other than the merchandise and lifestyle that money buys. We live in a self-serving continuous loop that enriches the few at the expense of everyone else. There is an unacknowledged sorrow in this way of living, which may be felt as alienation, anger, helplessness or a lack of meaning in one's life. I have found that life's meaning is directly related to the inner recognition of a deeper purpose to our existence and a rejection of any cultural imperative or institutional authority that interferes with seeing this for oneself.

If the dark night of the soul is "the preparation for great light," as John of the Cross suggested, there is also a hidden light in the sorrow that descends on us when a loved one dies. The experience of overwhelming loss can lead to an existential void and life-altering questions, such as: is there such a thing as divine love, God, sacred Silence or anything transcendent at all? Or are we just deluding ourselves? When sorrow overtakes us, nothing seems to make sense; life seems to be "a tale told by an idiot, full of sound and fury, signifying nothing," as Shakespeare wrote in Macbeth.

Losing someone dear to us can produce a spiritual crisis that nullifies the life we once had — a complete undoing of the known, temporarily hurling us into what seems like an abyss. I'm not speaking of the medical condition of depression, but a spiritual unmooring that exposes our helplessness in the upheaval of grief and sorrow. As mentioned earlier, grief can drive us into the depths of despair, but it can also awaken compassion for the totality of suffering throughout the world. If our own sorrow can open our hearts to others, then surely it is "the light that pierces the darkness."[38]

"Where there is sorrow, there is holy ground," wrote Oscar Wilde. "Someday people will realize what that means. They will know nothing of life till they do." Wilde wrote this sitting alone and isolated in his London prison cell, incarcerated for "gross indecency,"

the legal term at the time for simply being gay. As he reflected on his life up to that point and endured the hardships and humiliations of two years in prison, spiritual insights flowed from his sorrow. "I find hidden somewhere away in my nature something that tells me that nothing in the whole world is meaningless, and suffering least of all ... the silence, the solitude, the shame — each and all of these things I have to transform into a spiritual experience." His book length letter about what he learned in prison was published after his release. You can find Wilde's deeply personal exploration of sorrow in *De Profundis*, which is Latin for "from the depths."

The dark night urges us to discover the unseen causes of sorrow from the depths of our own anguish. This is very difficult because the most potent discoveries are often about fear, including the most terrorizing fear of all: the inevitability of our own death and the loss of everyone we love. There is simply no hiding from this truth even though nearly everything in modern culture covers it up or denies it. We separate life from aging and death despite the fact that living and dying are a continuum. We see it in nature, but ignore it in ourselves.

If our species, particularly those living in wealthy Western countries, openly acknowledged the certainty of bodily death, no matter how powerful, rich or famous one might be, the world might be more equitable and harmonious. There would be no need for death-denying advertising that ignores or devalues the elderly. We would honor the beauty and possibilities of every life passage — not only the radiance of youth, but also the valuable experience of the old. We could have an authentic media conversation about aging and death, and finally confront our collective obsession with power, wealth and celebrity. A life with integrity and compassion could actually be a topic worthy of discussion on cable news programs and social media.

But instead we are subjected to acrimonious shouting matches that pit one personality against another. The shallowness of our public discourse is corrosive to our collective state-of-mind, but it makes a lot of money. As long as the profit motive controls the airwaves and the Internet, the life experience of ordinary human beings, including the passage into death, will be ignored. Perhaps it is ignored because the contemplation of one's own death reveals, like nothing else can, that death makes us all equal. The denial of this fact makes us fools.

Elisabeth Kubler-Ross, a pioneer in bringing together dying and living in a way that has changed millions of lives, added invaluable perspective to the struggle we have with loss and sorrow. She wrote: "There are only two emotions: love and fear. But it's more accurate to say that there is only love or fear, for we cannot feel these two emotions together, at exactly the same time. When we're in a place of love, we cannot be in a place of fear."[39] Her profound insight came from many years of helping dying hospice patients and their families lovingly accept what each of us will face one day.

An experience of the dark night can also develop from grieving for a way of life that has died. For example, there is a great deal of personal and collective sorrow throughout the world caused by the impact of the Covid-19 pandemic. Millions of people have died and millions more have been hospitalized. Many Covid-19 survivors may have to endure a lifetime of side effects from the damage the virus does in the body. New phrases have been introduced into our everyday language, like "social distancing" and "stay-at-home orders." Travel restrictions, job loss, school closures, economic hardships and new variants of the virus add more uncertainty and sadness. Life has dramatically changed as a result of the pandemic. As I write this, some countries are doing much better, while others are in a worsening crisis. No matter where we live, there is no guarantee that life will ever be the same again. In this sense, we have been living in a global dark night that may have an impact for a generation.

There is also collective sorrow that is building around climate change and the exploitation of the Earth — grief for the beauty that is already lost in places like the Amazon rainforest, Antarctica, Greenland and other parts of the world. These irreparable losses remind us of our dependence on nature for our survival. As more people around the world awaken to the serious damage being done to the Earth's ecosystems and atmosphere, concern and sorrow widens, especially when people feel helpless about stopping it. But there is a positive aspect to this: there is now a growing awareness that our fate as a species is directly linked to how we treat wildlife and the natural world, and so a shift in human consciousness is possible.

Imagine for a moment that the entire content of human consciousness — which is derived from the consciousness of every human being on Earth — is inside an immense cloud or an enormous floating container that circulates above the Earth. Each person on the planet contributes the quality of his or her consciousness into this vast container. If you are angry, more anger is added. If you are kind, more kindness is added. The content of human consciousness is the sum total of what we individually contribute to the whole container. That is why the quality of your awareness is so important. You matter far more than you realize. For example, your patience balances anxiety. Your compassion mitigates hate. Your inner stillness diminishes fear. The realization that each of us is always contributing to the collective content of human consciousness can remake the world. In seeing this with the whole of one's being, the dark night of endless war, poverty and exploitation can finally stop, and the wisdom of the heart can take its rightful place in human affairs.

The wise and silent teaching that the dark night conveys is a heightened sensitivity to the suffering of others. And when there is sensitivity to the fate of others, there is the potential for a radical transformation in human affairs. The paradox of the dark night is that its sorrow can reveal the hidden light of our own wholeness, not as an intellectual theory, but as a living truth. In accepting our impermanence, not just intellectually, but down to the marrow of our bones, there is another revelation the dark night discloses. It is the truth that is as old as time, yet always new: while the physical form that life takes will die one day, love does not. Love is formless, silent and always present, when we are present.

The wise and silent teaching of the dark night is a heightened sensitivity to the suffering of others.

*The dark night can reveal the hidden light of our own
wholeness, not as an intellectual theory, but as a living truth.*

While the body will die one day, love does not. Love is formless, silent and always present, when we are present.

The realization that each of us is always contributing to the content of human consciousness can remake the world.

Death, loss and sorrow are woven into the fabric of life. And they are also lanterns by which we see into ourselves.

The dark night urges us to discover the hidden causes of sorrow from the depths of our own anguish.

To listen and see from within inner silence builds the bridge that transports us out of sorrow and to the shore of unconditioned love.

For all its excruciating inner challenges, the dark night can be a wisdom teacher.

17

Transformation

"Come into being as you pass away."
The Gospel of Thomas

Being aware of your own inner awareness is the beginning of self-transformation. The exploration in previous chapters of a more subtle awareness of listening and seeing helps us transcend, to some extent, our conditioned mind, so that we can be free of its limitations. In silent listening and seeing, the mind is empty of thought, at peace with itself and united with the wisdom of the heart. The old "me" has passed away and a new human being is born into a world that desperately needs more wisdom and compassion. This dimension of awareness is suggested by the statement in the Gospel of Thomas, "come into being as you pass away."

Our fundamental challenge is to be aware of the structure of the mind-made self because if we don't understand how our mind works, there can be no inner freedom and we are stuck in the repeating patterns of the past, without even realizing it. We sleep-walk through life, but believe we're awake. That is why exploring the awareness of alert listening and alert seeing has been emphasized in this book.

Only in *seeing* the truth of our dilemma can a transformation take place. If we inwardly see that the source of our discontent is the ever-talking egoic mind, along with our tendency to believe its chatter, we profoundly alter the way we see each other and the world. Gurdjieff expressed it this way: "Awakening begins when a man realizes that he is going nowhere and does not know where to go." We wake up to the uncomfortable fact that we do not know what we think we know. In admitting that we do not know, a new life begins: a life that may look the same on the outside, but is far more vibrant on the inside.

A new beginning such as this requires fearlessness because nearly everything in our society is hostile to the real change that ends division, tribalism and the trap of conformity. Sooner or later, we find out if we truly wish to break free or just want to talk about it like we talk about the weather. Is there a real willingness to sacrifice one's personal smallness and live with the questions rather than another person's answers? Krishnamurti phrased it this way: "Is there a light that is not lit by another?" This question, and what is implied by it, is one of the most important questions we can ask ourselves. It complements Ramana Maharshi's question: "Who am I?"

"I want to unfold. Let no place in me hold itself closed, for where I am closed, I am false," wrote Rainer Maria Rilke. To unfold is to learn what is true and what is false. This involves patience, self-inquiry and the friendship of inner silence. When the embrace of the wordless language of Silence envelops us, what is true is inwardly audible to us. There is an inner perception without an image — a seeing of the unseen. In learning to "come into being as you pass away," self-transformation happens effortlessly. It is the death of an imagined somebody. The same death is implied in the often quoted Sufi proverb: "die before you die." This suggests dying to yesterday and all previous yesterdays, dying to all tomorrows, and to the illusion of "me" and "other." Then there is a radical transformation.

In the natural world, there are some transformations which are truly remarkable. One of the most fascinating occurs in the life of a dragonfly. After its birth from an egg, a dragonfly nymph looks like a rather ugly six-legged spider. It crawls on the bottom of muddy ponds and lakes for months, while its body evolves through a series of inner transformations in the murky depths. It grows out of one body and into another body several times during its underwater lifespan. Eventually it leaves its watery abode, where it breathed like a fish through gills, and rises to the water's surface with newly evolved lungs that breathe the same air we do. Then it crawls onto land and rests on a leaf, a flower or a bush. The dragonfly then begins its final metamorphosis as it vacates its body one last time and is reborn into something entirely new. It is transformed from a bottom-feeding water creature to a dazzling airborne beauty that bathes in sunlight. It is one of the most startling transformations in the natural world.

The dragonfly is a beautiful and enigmatic creature steeped in mythological and spiritual symbolism, particularly in Asian and Native American cultures. Its exquisite iridescent wings magically reflect and refract sunlight, creating the illusion that it changes color with the intensity of light. The numerous transformations of a dragonfly and the dance of light on its celestial wings have prompted poets and artists from around the world to depict it as a symbol of spiritual transformation and a messenger from above. The dragonfly has come to represent the transformative human journey from the darkness of ignorance to the light of inner freedom. It is also a symbol of regeneration and renewal.

But unlike the dragonfly, whose stunning transformation occurs on nature's biological cue, a human being must actually be aware of the need for self-transformation and then voluntarily make the sacrifice that is necessary to be inwardly free. While it is true that spiritual transformation can happen instantly in moment-to-moment awareness, it is also true that sages and saints prepared themselves for their own transformation, just as we must. From Lao Tzu, to Francis of Assisi, to Pema Chödrön, the preparatory inner work that opens us to a unitary state of being and a deep awareness of compassion is given to those who learn to sacrifice what they are *not* without expecting anything. And so it is the quality of one's awareness that determines spiritual unfoldment. "Seek and ye shall find; knock and the door will open," said the Christ in the Gospel of Matthew, suggesting a dimension of awareness in which we see with newly awakened eyes that the world is only a reflection of ourselves. As we change, so does the world. In that sense, each one of us is the possibility of the transformation of the human race.

"If you begin to understand what you are without trying to change it, then what you are undergoes a transformation," said Krishnamurti throughout his life. And of course, we see what we are in the light of non-judgmental self-observation with the help of alert listening and seeing. Essentially, we undergo a transformation when we realize that the conditioned mind is in the way of what we seek, and then begin the inner work of understanding it and transcending it. It doesn't mean we're suddenly flawless human beings — life goes on as before, but by gaining insight into who we are, there is more inner silence to *see* ourselves and the world with compassion. Life may be difficult at times, but whatever happens, we can view it as a wisdom teaching because how we respond tells us what we're made of in any given moment. The more inner quietude that is present, the greater our capacity to be at ease with what is. "When I am silent, I fall into that place where everything is music," wrote Rumi.

When Rumi speaks of falling into a place where "everything is music," he suggests an effortless letting go and a mind completely at rest. A mind at rest is not thinking; it is very quiet. And that brings us back to the awareness we bring to listening and seeing. By learning to rest the mind in silence, no matter how brief the silence may be, we may "fall" gently and effortlessly into a direct experience of the Silence in which we are fully awake to ourselves and to the rest of creation.

*We undergo a transformation when we realize
that what we seek is already within us.*

18

Living in Awareness
Awareness Suggestion #5

"I saw an angel in the marble and carved until I could set him free."
Michelangelo

Our exploration together has centered on what stands in the way of inner freedom and a more meaningful life — the fog of conditioning that distorts our perception of ourselves, others and the world. It is this inability to see our conditioning that prevents us from understanding the causes of our psychological suffering. But there is a more subtle form of awareness that sees clearly. This perceiving awareness is the act of self-observation without judgment, and it occurs in the relaxed attention of alert seeing and listening. When our ingrained thought patterns are recognized for what they are, it is this very recognition that quiets the mind. And when the mind is very still, we may glimpse the bliss at the root of our being. To quote Thomas Merton once again, it is "the hidden ground of love for which there is no explanation."

Spanish poet, Juan Ramón Jiménez — beautifully translated into English by Robert Bly — wrote a poem that suggests the immensity and the closeness of Silence. The poem is called, "I am not I." Jiménez describes walking with an "I" that he does not see, and yet he is inwardly aware of its gentle, forgiving and silent Presence. He contrasts this loving Presence with his own tendency not to love.

The invisible "I" who walks with him is actually *within* him – not separate from him, and its mysterious beauty is beyond time. He calls it the, I "who will remain standing when I die."

One way to glimpse the dimension of awareness that Jiménez refers to is to give attention to alert seeing and listening. I know this has been emphasized throughout the book, but frequent reminders are needed because a state of inner awareness comes and goes for most of us. Remembering that we can return again and again to an attentive, quiet way of seeing and listening is an important part of staying awake in the hypnosis of a frenzied world.

The awareness suggestion I'm about to describe is a simple meditative walk in which the movement of your body, the impressions of your surroundings, the content of your mind, and your response to that content are observed with relaxed attention.

There is nothing you have to achieve and no destination you have to reach — you are simply taking a walk with a seeing and listening awareness that receives the sensory impressions of walking, and observes them without judgment. In this way, you are aware of your inner awareness, as well as the automatic aspects of listening and seeing at the superficial level. If the mind talks, it is merely part of your observation. Thoughts will arise of course. Sometimes it may even seem like you're listening to the dialogue of a Broadway play and all the characters in the play are you! A walk in the awareness of alert listening and seeing can show us how easily we fall into the habits of the talking mind. When that is seen, we have some freedom.

The suggestion is to take a five to ten minute walk in nature, in a park, or in your own neighborhood, and to be aware of what occurs, without judging it. Most of us will get distracted by thoughts within a minute or two. The talking mind will chatter on about something. Observe it as you walk and take in what you see. That's it. No worries, no stress, no wanting anything — just watch what happens. If walking outdoors is not possible due to weather or a physical condition, you can try this awareness suggestion at home by adapting it to your circumstances. Whether you are inside or outside, whether you walk or sit, the point is to realize that our everyday activities can be a rich inquiry into the quality of our awareness or our lack of awareness. This can be healing if you give it your attention.

Begin by wearing comfortable clothing and shoes. But before you take your walk, sit quietly for a few minutes and be aware of your breath. Take a few minutes to settle into a comfortable breathing rhythm. As you breathe, notice the rising and falling of your diaphragm. If it's comfortable for you, place your right hand on your chest, so that the palm of your hand is resting gently near your heart. Relax your arms and shoulders and breathe in your normal way.

After a minute or two of noticing the rhythm of the rise and fall of your chest, you may feel the beating of your heart resonating in the palm of your hand. It may take a minute before you become aware of this, and it may be very subtle. You may not notice anything at all. This isn't a test. It's simply a way to be in contact with the aliveness of your body. And it can calm the mind because your attention is on your breath, the rising and falling of your chest, and the resonance of your own heartbeat. There is a universe within you and at the center of this inner universe is your heart.

By taking a few minutes to sit quietly in the awareness of your breath, there is a greater possibility that your walk will have more inner silence. After a few minutes of relaxation and when it feels comfortable, you can begin your walk in the place of your choosing. If you wish to walk with another person, it's helpful if both of you agree to make the attempt to walk in the awareness of alert listening and seeing. Having a walking partner who shares your interest in exploring the perceiving awareness of self-observation can help each of you sustain this mutual inquiry. You can silently remind each other to stay awake. But this is not necessary. In this awareness walk, you are your own wisdom teacher. The quality of your own listening and seeing conveys the teaching, whether you walk alone or not.

Once you are outside and ready to go on your walk, stand still for a moment and listen with relaxed attention. What do you hear? What do you see? Your mind will label what you see and hear as, "tree," "car," "barking dog," "lawn mower," or "blue sky." Whatever the mind names, it is just a name. Let the naming come and go.

As you take your first step, notice the movement of raising your leg and placing one foot in front of the other. Notice how your head turns when observing something to the left or the right. Be aware of inhaling the air. The body does this on its own, but now you are aware of what the body is doing — the motion of your legs and feet, the bending of the knee, the action of your arms, the feeling in your thighs, the sensation of your feet touching the surface you walk on, the rush of impressions that enter through all your senses, and the thoughts and feelings that arise with them.

There is a tremendous amount of attentive energy as you quietly walk in alert seeing and listening, if you have not slipped into passive listening and seeing — the "sleep" of our ordinary state of consciousness. This happens to all of us. But the second you notice your inattention, a new connection forms between your mind and body. Your relationship to what you see and hear is now alive with wakefulness because you witness what occurs in yourself and in your surroundings from a deeper dimension of awareness.

You may wonder why this matters — after all it's just an ordinary walk and nothing really happens. Actually something extraordinary happens. In giving your attention freely and fully, you are aware of the awareness in life itself. Life is permeated with Silent Awareness — you *are* that. The attention of alert listening and seeing gives you a glimpse of what it may mean to be truly awake to the power and sensitivity of your own inner being.

And this brings you much closer to the loving Presence that has always been within you — the, I AM beyond time and space, and made of love.

19

Song of the Canyon
The Wisdom of the Wilderness

*"I only went out for a walk and finally concluded to stay out till
sundown, for going out, I found, was really going in."*

John Muir

The first time I saw the Grand Canyon was on a cold, clear
morning in January. It was the type of encounter with the
natural world that ignites a flash of wonder and bestows
reverence. Fresh fallen snow covered canyon peaks like a soft, wooly
blanket. Limbs of tall, fragrant pine trees glistened brightly in their
garments of snow and ice. A large raven plunged into the canyon
from a hidden perch, flew high, then out of sight.

From the canyon's South Rim, I watched the rising sun play a
silent symphony of light and shadow that magically traveled over
massive red rock walls. My knees nearly buckled as I stood in awe of
stunning, never-ending vistas. The immensity of silence enfolded
everything — the cliffs, the sky, the Earth, the air, and the smallness
of me. I went out to see the canyon in early morning light, and in a
moment of absolute stillness, no "me" was there, only the seeing.

What came later was the insight that the natural world can be our
partner in self-transformation, if we honor it, care for it and listen to

its unspoken wisdom. Protecting the wilderness and being in harmony with the profound silence of Earth's majestic places nurtures and renews us. It's medicine for the soul. This is the lesson I learned at the Grand Canyon many years ago.

The Grand Canyon has been called "the womb of the earth" by Native Americans because of a creation story that depicts the emergence of the material world out of its inner depths. To pueblo Indian tribes of Northern Arizona, the Grand Canyon is sacred ground, a land where deities brought forth the origin of time and where ancestral spirits dwell. For the Hopi, the Grand Canyon is a place where life, death and eternity meet and co-exist. It is said that their ancestors emerged from its depths, and after death, their departed spirits went to live among the towering rock formations at the root of the world. Thus life and death are not separate, but one dynamic continuum with its source in an invisible realm. A Hopi woman told me that they continually send prayers into the Grand Canyon to protect its life-affirming beauty.

That first visit twenty-five years ago was in winter, when there are far fewer tourists because the weather can be challenging, but I was happy to trade cold weather for some measure of solitude with the canyon. This came at a time when I was trying to integrate four years of photographing wounded children during the Balkan War with my everyday life in the suburbs, where I lived at the time. The experience of war changes a person — whether you are a combatant, a medic, a journalist or a humanitarian truck driver bringing medicine and food to those who need it — war rearranges the psyche and the tolerance for the status-quo, at least it did in my case. The old life, which had always included a spiritual dimension, was no longer valid and I was also physically and emotionally worn out.

I needed to rest and rejuvenate somewhere in nature, but my usual retreat destinations — the Pacific ocean or California's redwood and sequoia forests did not seem like a good fit, probably because they were so familiar. In the middle of a sleepless night an inner prompting arose — "Grand Canyon." I had never been there before, but the impulse to go was strong, so I booked a cabin for two weeks on the South Rim, and got in the car for the ten hour drive to northern Arizona. Back then, many cabins at the Grand Canyon were rustic with no television, Internet or the constant distractions of today's mobile devices. It's hard to imagine now, but the digital world as we know it today was not part of daily life twenty-five years ago.

Each morning before sunrise I found a spot near the canyon's edge and sat down to enjoy the quietude of the rising sun. Wrapped in a wool blanket and wearing two pairs of socks to keep my feet from freezing, I sat with eyes closed and let the first rays of sun warm my face. Then I watched morning light sweep across a magnificent landscape as vibrant colors of red and orange, once hidden in night's shadow, burst into bloom with daylight. I was invigorated by the sights and sounds of one of the greatest natural wonders in the world.

Witnessing the canyon wake up from its slumber at daybreak was the best part of my day — an hour of being with a cherished new friend who gave me joy, strength and vitality in exchange for simply being there. This was a startling revelation because there seemed to be a mysterious play of energies between me and the canyon — between my attention and the primeval presence that makes the Grand Canyon what it is. It became clear to me that the Grand Canyon is alive. It has power and purpose beyond my capacity to understand or describe. And it can communicate — not with words of course, but through color, sound, light, shadow and with its immense spaciousness.

Perhaps the language of the Grand Canyon might be the vibration of the Earth itself, a sacred song composed only for ears that can hear it. It may not be quantifiable by science, but it can be discerned by an ancient people like the Hopi. There are rock formations in the Grand Canyon that are over two billion years old. To native peoples, geologists and anthropologists, they help tell the story of the Earth and its ancient inhabitants. The canyon's rocks are not inert or lifeless. They are a living presence. People from all over the world visit there, not only to see the marvels of it, but to experience the mystery of creation and silently contemplate its stupendous natural beauty untouched by man. And it must stay that way. Its raw power to inspire and heal is the canyon's gift to humanity.

When I was tired of my own turbulence, I gazed in awe at its astounding heights and depths and felt its silent force. Then I hiked down the canyon to see if it would unveil its secret. But the unveiling that took place was in me. That is what a quiet place in nature helps to facilitate — the unmasking of ourselves to ourselves.

Spending a week with the Being of the Grand Canyon brought perspective and equilibrium. In the expanse of its ancient red rock cathedrals and on the hallowed ground of its native people, I saw that I was living in a small portion of myself, governed by thoughts that left out the astounding goodness I had seen in the selfless courage of volunteers who traveled to a war zone, at great personal risk, to mitigate suffering. They came from all parts of the world to make a difference, and they did. I realized that the sadness that burdened me after every visit to a frontline hospital or refugee camp was partnered with the compassion I witnessed of many caring and generous people. There was great beauty in that — the counterpoint to sorrow.

Our species moves between two poles: beauty and ugliness, tenderness and cruelty, love and fear. It's the fact of the conditioned, egoic mind, but we have the capacity to be in communion with a much deeper awareness that brings us peace. Everything you need to know is available to you right now. Take a conscious breath, rest your weary mind, and be at ease in this moment. The loving wholeness you seek is always within you.

The Silence that is infinite waits for you
to recognize it as your own.

Silent Awareness gathers our scattered parts
and makes us whole.

If you have a sincere wish to be inwardly silent,
begin with the simple act of listening.

There is no greater mystery than Silent Awareness.

*It has always been your beloved companion
even if you are unaware of its Presence.*

You are the Light that dispels the darkness.

The loving wholeness you seek
is always within you.
Rest your mind in quietude.

With Gratitude

Spiritual inquiry brings us together in subtle and profound ways. We help each other in times of challenge or confusion, sometimes without even realizing it. To friends and colleagues near and far: thank you for your support and wisdom — you have made the inner journey more accessible and less lonely.

I would like to express heartfelt appreciation to all the participants who have attended my workshops and retreats over the last two decades. Settling into interior silence with a group of caring people who value its transformative possibilities is a powerful reminder of our true relationship with each other. Thank you for encouraging me to present a straightforward approach to recovering the inner awareness that brings equilibrium to a turbulent world.

I'd also like to express gratitude to my editor, Letitia Grimes, for her loving attention to the text and for her many helpful suggestions. Her contributions enhance the book.

And to Gabriele Uhlein, who wrote the foreword — her contemplative life is an inspiration to me and many others. I am grateful for her encouragement and her wise and compassionate heart.

About The Author

Cynthia facilitates retreats and offers workshops that focus on self-transformation and the importance of inwardly perceiving ourselves and the world with compassion. This perceiving awareness silently sees that there is no "other."

Drawing from the world's great wisdom teachings and her own insights, she presents a way of listening and seeing with the inner awareness that arises in stillness. She has come to see that a truly quiet mind is a non-violent mind. Her commitment to contributing to a more compassionate world is shaped by many years of spiritual inquiry and by her experience of war. During the Balkan War, she worked with United Nations humanitarian organizations as a photojournalist in frontline hospitals, where she photographed war wounded children to help bring awareness to their suffering. With the help of some wonderful people, she was able to bring one wounded child to the United States for medical care that saved his leg from amputation.

Cynthia's lifelong inquiry into the transformative possibilities of inner stillness combined with personally seeing the effects of war on children is what motivates her to write and speak about the urgent need for a radical change in human consciousness. Without such a change, we may not have a sustainable planet to live on much longer, and there will be even more global division, war, and poverty. Her mission is to help facilitate a greater awakening of our true relationship with each other and the natural world, and to help bring about a transformation that can save us from ourselves.

For more information: www.cynthiaoverweg.com

End Notes

[1] *Nisargadatta Maharaj, I Am That: Talks with Sri Nisargadatta Maharaj,* translated by Maurice Frydman; revised and edited by Sudhakar Dikshit (Durham, NC: The Acorn Press, 2020) 1st US ed., 1982. 2d ed. 2012, 3rd impression 2020, pp.374-5.

[2] Thomas Merton, *The Hidden Ground of Love: Letters on Religious Experience and Social Concerns,* edited by William H. Shannon, Harcourt, Brace, Jovanovich, 1993, p. 115.

[3] Dante Alighieri, *The Divine Comedy,* translated by John Ciardi, New American Library a division of Penguin Books, 2003, pp.892-894.

[4] *The Dalai Lama A Policy of Kindness: An Anthology of Writings By and About the Dalai Lama,* compiled by Sidney Piburn, Snow Lion, 1993, p.52.

[5] *Krishnamurti's Notebook,* Krishnamurti Foundation of America and Krishnamurti Foundation Trust, Full Text Edition, 2003, pp. 205-6.

Content reproduced by permission. Permission to quote from the works of J. Krishnamurti or other works for which the copyright is held by the Krishnamurti Foundation of America or the Krishnamurti Foundation Trust Ltd has been given on the understanding that such permission does not indicate endorsement of the views expressed in this media.

[6] *Krishnamurti to Himself,* HarperCollins, 1993, p.18.

[7] www.population.un.org/wpp/Publications/Files/WPP2019_10KeyFindings.pdf

[8] www.unhcr.org/climate-change-and-disasters.html

[9] Poona India 4th Public Talk 19th September, 1948.
https://jkrishnamurti.org/content/poona-india-4th-public-talk-19th-september-1948

[10] www.dalailama.com/messages/compassion-and-human-values/compassion

[11] www.dalailama.com

[12] *Bhagavad-Gita: The Song of God,* translated by Swami Prabhavananda and Christopher Isherwood, New American Library, 1951.

[13] Matthew 16:24

[14] Rainer Maria Rilke, *Rilke's Book of Hours: Love Poems to God,* translated by Anita Barrows and Joanna Macy, Riverhead Books, 1997, p.116

[15] *The Upanishads: Breath of the Eternal,* translated by Swami Prabhavananda and Frederick Manchester, New American Library, Mentor Edition, 1948, pp. 46-47.

[16] *Nisargadatta Maharaj, I Am That: Talks with Sri Nisargadatta Maharaj,* translated by Maurice Frydman; revised and edited by Sudhakar Dikshit (Durham, NC: The Acorn Press, 2020) 1st US ed., 1982. 2d ed. 2012, 3rd impression 2020. *Content reproduced by permission from the publisher.*

[17] Antoine de Saint-Exupéry, *The Little Prince,* Harcourt, Inc. 2000.

[18] Matthew 5:7

[19] *Doorkeeper of the Heart: Versions of Rabi'a,* Charles Upton, Pir Press, 2004. http://www.rabiainstitute.org/rabia-al-basri/

[20] H.P. Blavatsky, *The Voice of the Silence,* Theosophical Publishing House, 1992.

[21] *The Essential Teachings of Ramana Maharshi: A Visual Journey,* Inner Directions, 2003, p.69.

[22] Corinthians 6:19

[23] Eknath Easwaran, *The Upanishads,* Nilgiri Press, 2007, p.223.

[24] Mary Oliver, *Upstream: Selected Essays*, Penguin Press, 2016.

[25] Sri Ramana Maharshi, W*ho Am I*, Sai ePublications, 2021

[26] Peter Wohlleben, *The Hidden Life of Trees: What They Feel, How They Communicate – Discoveries from a Secret World,* Greystone Books, 2016.

[27] Matthew 16:24

[28] Genesis 1

[29] Genesis 2.7

[30] Edgar Mitchell with Dwight Williams, Th*e Way of the Explorer*, G.P. Putnam's Sons, 1996, p.59

[31] Ezekiel 18:31

[32] www.dalailama.com/messages/compassion-and-human-values/compassion

[33] *Dark Night of the Soul: St. John of the Cross,* translated by E. Allison Peers, from the original critical edition of P. Silverio de Santa Teresa, OCD, Dover Publications, New York, 1953, p.2

[34] *The Collected Works of St. John of the Cross,* translated by Kieran Kavanaugh, OCD and Otilio Rodriguez, OCD, ICS Publications, Revised Edition, 1991, p.471

[35] John 3:3

[36] Teresa of Avila, *The Life of St. Teresa of Avila by Herself*, Penguin Classics, 1988.

[37] *Man's Search for Meaning,* Viktor Frankl, Touchstone, Simon & Shuster, 1984.

[38] John 1:5

[39] Elisabeth Kubler-Ross and David Kessler, *Life Lessons: Two Experts on Death and Dying Teach Us About the Mysteries of Life and Living,* Scribner, updated edition 2014.

Printed in Great Britain
by Amazon

24483728R00101